Muffins In A Jar

♥

Muffin Recipes for Ingredients in a Jar

Lia Rossner Wilson

Muffins In a Jar

1st Printing   April 2005

ISBN 1-931294-89-5
Library of Congress 2005920232

Illustrated by Nancy Murphy Griffith
Manufactured in China
Designed in the United States of America by
Cookbook Resources, LLC
541 Doubletree Drive
Highland Village, Texas 75077
Toll free 866-229-2665
www.cookbookresources.com

Contents

YOUR GIFT JARS
CAN BE SPECTACULAR

Dressing up your gift jar is limited only by your imagination, so have fun! This is an excellent craft project for older children, and even the little ones can help paint, glue and decorate. Gather your supplies and enjoy some time together. With fabric, ribbon, and colored pens you can quickly and inexpensively personalize your gift jars for that special person or occasion.

TOP IT!

Ideas:

- Paint lid and decorate with buttons, charms, shells, beads or old costume jewelry.

- Lace Doilies: Place $6^{1}/_{2}$ to 7-inch doily over a painted lid or solid color circle of fabric. You may be able to lace ribbon through and tie in a bow.

- Brown craft paper (brown paper bag) cut in a $6^{1}/_{2}$ to 7-inch circle. This looks very country if tied with natural or red raffia.

- Fabric cut in $6^{1}/_{2}$ to 7-inch circle or 2, $6^{1}/_{2}$ to 7-inch squares of coordinating fabric. Place the first square on top of the second so that the points are centered on the straight edge. The catty-corner placement produces a cute handkerchief hem.

Pointers:

- Cutting with pinking shears or fancy edge scissors will finish the edge nicely. Use a pencil to trace a $6^{1}/_{2}$ to 7-inch circle or square on the wrong side of your fabric. A plate or lid works well for a quick pattern. If you are making more than one topper, you will want to layer as many fabrics as your scissors will comfortably cut. Pin your layers together and cut.

- Edges of lace, fringe, or beading may be applied by either sewing or gluing.

- Center the topper on jar lid and secure with a rubber band.

TIE IT!

Ideas:

✂ Ribbon   ✂ Wired Ribbon   ✂ Jute   ✂ Cording   ✂ Raffia

✂ Narrow ribbon-use several strands of the same or complimentary colors.

✂ Weave a ribbon through straight or ruffled lace and tie in a bow. If using straight lace cut it twice the length to go around the lid.

✂ Decorative wire garland (stars, snowflakes, hearts etc.)- wrap wire around the lid several times and twist to secure. If you leave a tail of 6 inches on both sides, you can curl them by coiling the wire around a pencil.

Pointers:

• Slant-cut ends of streamers.

• Fold ribbon edges together lengthwise and cut a slant from edge up toward the fold. This technique gives you a two-pointed tail on the streamer.

• Knot each ribbon streamer a couple of times at different intervals. This is an attractive look when using several strands of narrow ribbons.

• Knot only the ends of each streamer. It's a great look for jute or cording.

• Tie small jingle bells, buttons or charms to each streamer.

• Loop a couple of small tassels around cording.

TAG IT!

Each recipe has 6 tags, which include baking instructions.

🏷 Photocopy or simply cut apart and attach to jar.

🏷 Use colored pens to add a little zip.

🏷 There is plenty of room for a greeting or use one of the friendship quotes from the book. In a hurry? Use tag with a pre-printed greeting.

" *May* there always be work for your hands to do, may your purse always hold a coin or two. May the sun always shine on your windowpane, may a rainbow be certain to follow each rain. May the hand of a friend always be near you, may God fill your heart with gladness to cheer you."

~Irish Blessing

Best Bran Muffins

Best Bran Muffins

Ingredients for Jar:
1 cup flour
1 tablespoon baking powder
$1/2$ teaspoon salt
$1^1/2$ cups bran cereal
$1/2$ cup sugar
$1/2$ cup raisins
$1/2$ cup coarsely chopped walnuts

Instructions for Jar:

1. Mix flour with baking powder and salt.

2. Put flour in bottom of 1-quart jar and layer remaining
   ingredients in following order: bran cereal, sugar, raisins,
   walnuts.

3. Place lid on jar, close and attach baking instructions.

♥ Decorate your jar using the suggestions found
   on pages 4 and 5.

Best Bran Muffins

Instructions for baking:

1 cup milk
1 egg, slightly beaten
$^1/_4$ cup ($^1/_2$ stick) butter, melted

1. Preheat oven to 400°.

2. Empty contents of jar into large bowl and stir to mix.

3. In separate bowl, whisk milk, egg and melted butter and blend well.

4. Add liquid mixture to dry mixture and stir until just moist.

5. Spoon batter into 12 prepared muffin cups.

6. Bake for 20 minutes or until tester comes out clean.

"*The glory of friendship is not the outstretched hand nor the kindly smile nor the joy of companionship; it is the spiritual inspiration that comes to one when he discovers that someone else believes in him and is willing to trust him.* "

~Ralph Waldo Emerson

Best Bran Muffins
Instructions for baking:
1 cup milk
1 egg, slightly beaten
$^1/_4$ cup ($^1/_2$ stick) butter, melted

1. Preheat oven to 400°.
2. Empty contents of jar into large bowl and stir to mix.
3. In separate bowl, whisk milk, egg and melted butter and blend well.
4. Add liquid mixture to dry mixture and stir until just moist.
5. Spoon batter into 12 prepared muffin cups.
6. Bake for 20 minutes or until tester comes out clean.

www.cookbookresources.com

- ✂

Best Bran Muffins
Instructions for baking:
1 cup milk
1 egg, slightly beaten
$^1/_4$ cup ($^1/_2$ stick) butter, melted

1. Preheat oven to 400°.
2. Empty contents of jar into large bowl and stir to mix.
3. In separate bowl, whisk milk, egg and melted butter and blend well.
4. Add liquid mixture to dry mixture and stir until just moist.
5. Spoon batter into 12 prepared muffin cups.
6. Bake for 20 minutes or until tester comes out clean.

www.cookbookresources.com

- -

Best Bran Muffins
Instructions for baking:
1 cup milk
1 egg, slightly beaten
$^1/_4$ cup ($^1/_2$ stick) butter, melted

1. Preheat oven to 400°.
2. Empty contents of jar into large bowl and stir to mix.
3. In separate bowl, whisk milk, egg and melted butter and blend well.
4. Add liquid mixture to dry mixture and stir until just moist.
5. Spoon batter into 12 prepared muffin cups.
6. Bake for 20 minutes or until tester comes out clean.

www.cookbookresources.com

Best Bran Muffins

Instructions for baking:

1 cup milk
1 egg, slightly beaten
$^1/_4$ cup ($^1/_2$ stick) butter, melted

1. Preheat oven to 400°.
2. Empty contents of jar into large bowl and stir to mix.
3. In separate bowl, whisk milk, egg and melted butter and blend well.
4. Add liquid mixture to dry mixture and stir until just moist.
5. Spoon batter into 12 prepared muffin cups.
6. Bake for 20 minutes or until tester comes out clean.

Best Bran Muffins

Instructions for baking:

1 cup milk
1 egg, slightly beaten
$^1/_4$ cup ($^1/_2$ stick) butter, melted

1. Preheat oven to 400°.
2. Empty contents of jar into large bowl and stir to mix.
3. In separate bowl, whisk milk, egg and melted butter and blend well.
4. Add liquid mixture to dry mixture and stir until just moist.
5. Spoon batter into 12 prepared muffin cups.
6. Bake for 20 minutes or until tester comes out clean.

Best Bran Muffins

Instructions for baking:

1 cup milk
1 egg, slightly beaten
$^1/_4$ cup ($^1/_2$ stiok) butter, melted

1. Preheat oven to 400°.
2. Empty contents of jar into large bowl and stir to mix.
3. In separate bowl, whisk milk, egg and melted butter and blend well.
4. Add liquid mixture to dry mixture and stir until just moist.
5. Spoon batter into 12 prepared muffin cups.
6. Bake for 20 minutes or until tester comes out clean.

Orange-Date-Nut Muffins

Orange-Date-Nut Muffins

Ingredients for Jar:

$^3/_4$ cup sugar
1 teaspoon cinnamon
$1^1/_2$ cups flour
2 tablespoons dried, grated orange peel
1 teaspoon baking powder
1 teaspoon baking soda
$^1/_2$ teaspoon salt
1 cup chopped dates
$^3/_4$ cup coarsely chopped walnuts

Instructions for Jar:

1. Combine sugar and cinnamon, mix completely and place in bottom of 1-quart jar.

2. Combine flour, orange peel, baking powder, baking soda and salt. Gently spoon over sugar mixture.

3. Place dates in even layer over sugar mixture.

4. Place walnuts over dates.

5. Place lid on jar, close and attach baking instructions.

Orange-Date-Nut Muffins

Instructions for baking:

$^1/_2$ cup (1 stick) butter, melted
1 egg, slightly beaten
$^3/_4$ cup orange juice

1. Preheat oven to 375°.

2. Empty contents of jar into large bowl and stir to mix.

3. In separate bowl, whisk melted butter, egg and orange juice and blend well.

4. Add liquid mixture to dry mixture and stir until just moist.

5. Spoon batter into 12 prepared muffin cups.

6. Bake for 18 to 20 minutes or until tester comes out clean.

"Far away there in the sunshine are my highest aspirations. I may not reach them, but I can look up and see their beauty, believe in them and try to follow where they may lead."

~Louisa May Alcott

Orange-Date-Nut Muffins
Instructions for baking:
$1/2$ cup (1 stick) butter, melted
1 egg, slightly beaten
$3/4$ cup orange juice

1. Preheat oven to 375°.
2. Empty contents of jar into large bowl and stir to mix.
3. In separate bowl, whisk melted butter, egg and orange juice and blend well.
4. Add liquid mixture to dry mixture and stir until just moist.
5. Spoon batter into 12 prepared muffin cups.
6. Bake for 18 to 20 minutes or until tester comes out clean.

Orange-Date-Nut Muffins
Instructions for baking:
$1/2$ cup (1 stick) butter, melted
1 egg, slightly beaten
$3/4$ cup orange juice

1. Preheat oven to 375°.
2. Empty contents of jar into large bowl and stir to mix.
3. In separate bowl, whisk melted butter, egg and orange juice and blend well.
4. Add liquid mixture to dry mixture and stir until just moist.
5. Spoon batter into 12 prepared muffin cups.
6. Bake for 18 to 20 minutes or until tester comes out clean.

www.cookbookresources.com

Orange-Date-Nut Muffins
Instructions for baking:
$1/2$ cup (1 stick) butter, melted
1 egg, slightly beaten
$3/4$ cup orange juice

1. Preheat oven to 375°.
2. Empty contents of jar into large bowl and stir to mix.
3. In separate bowl, whisk melted butter, egg and orange juice and blend well.
4. Add liquid mixture to dry mixture and stir until just moist.
5. Spoon batter into 12 prepared muffin cups.
6. Bake for 18 to 20 minutes or until tester comes out clean.

www.cookbookresources.com

Orange-Date-Nut Muffins
Instructions for baking:
½ cup (1 stick) butter, melted
1 egg, slightly beaten
¾ cup orange juice

1. Preheat oven to 375°.
2. Empty contents of jar into large bowl and stir to mix.
3. In separate bowl, whisk melted butter, egg and orange juice and blend well.
4. Add liquid mixture to dry mixture and stir until just moist.
5. Spoon batter into 12 prepared muffin cups.
6. Bake for 18 to 20 minutes or until tester comes out clean.

- ✂

Orange-Date-Nut Muffins
Instructions for baking:
½ cup (1 stick) butter, melted
1 egg, slightly beaten
¾ cup orange juice

1. Preheat oven to 375°.
2. Empty contents of jar into large bowl and stir to mix.
3. In separate bowl, whisk melted butter, egg and orange juice and blend well.
4. Add liquid mixture to dry mixture and stir until just moist.
5. Spoon batter into 12 prepared muffin cups.
6. Bake for 18 to 20 minutes or until tester comes out clean.

- ✂

Orange-Date-Nut Muffins
Instructions for baking:
½ cup (1 stick) butter, melted
1 egg, slightly beaten
¾ cup orange juice

1. Preheat oven to 375°.
2. Empty contents of jar into large bowl and stir to mix.
3. In separate bowl, whisk melted butter, egg and orange juice and blend well.
4. Add liquid mixture to dry mixture and stir until just moist.
5. Spoon batter into 12 prepared muffin cups.
6. Bake for 18 to 20 minutes or until tester comes out clean.

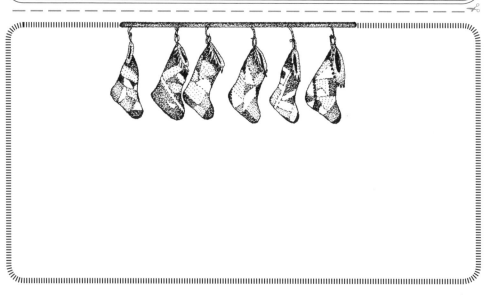

Cherry-Nut Muffins

Cherry-Nut Muffins

Ingredients for Jar:
2 cups flour
2 teaspoons baking powder
$3/4$ cup packed brown sugar
1 cup dried, sweetened cherries
$1/2$ cup chopped pecans

Instructions for Jar:
1. Combine flour and baking powder. Spoon mixture into bottom of 1-quart jar.

2. Gently spoon brown sugar in even layer over flour.

3. Layer cherries over brown sugar and pecans over cherries.

4. Place lid on jar, close and attach baking instructions.

♥ Decorate your jar using the suggestions found on pages 4 and 5.

Cherry-Nut Muffins

Instructions for baking:

2 eggs, slightly beaten
$2/3$ cup orange juice
$1/3$ cup vegetable oil

1. Preheat oven to 375°.

2. Empty contents of jar into large bowl and stir to mix.

3. In separate bowl, whisk eggs, orange juice and vegetable oil and blend well.

4. Add liquid mixture to dry mixture and stir until mixture is just moist.

5. Spoon batter into prepared muffin cups.

6. Bake for 20 minutes or until light brown.

*" A hug is a great gift.
One size fits all,
it can be given for any occasion
and it's easy to exchange."*
~Anonymous

Cherry-Nut Muffins
Instructions for baking:
2 eggs, slightly beaten
$^2/_3$ cup orange juice
$^1/_3$ cup vegetable oil

1. Preheat oven to 375°.
2. Empty contents of jar into large bowl and stir to mix.
3. In separate bowl, whisk eggs, orange juice and vegetable oil and blend well.
4. Add liquid mixture to dry mixture and stir until mixture is just moist.
5. Spoon batter into prepared muffin cups.
6. Bake for 20 minutes or until light brown.

- ✂

Cherry-Nut Muffins
Instructions for baking:
2 eggs, slightly beaten
$^2/_3$ cup orange juice
$^1/_3$ cup vegetable oil

1. Preheat oven to 375°.
2. Empty contents of jar into large bowl and stir to mix.
3. In separate bowl, whisk eggs, orange juice and vegetable oil and blend well.
4. Add liquid mixture to dry mixture and stir until mixture is just moist.
5. Spoon batter into prepared muffin cups.
6. Bake for 20 minutes or until light brown.

- ✂

Cherry-Nut Muffins
Instructions for baking:
2 eggs, slightly beaten
$^2/_3$ cup orange juice
$^1/_3$ cup vegetable oil

1. Preheat oven to 375°.
2. Empty contents of jar into large bowl and stir to mix.
3. In separate bowl, whisk eggs, orange juice and vegetable oil and blend well.
4. Add liquid mixture to dry mixture and stir until mixture is just moist.
5. Spoon batter into prepared muffin cups.
6. Bake for 20 minutes or until light brown.

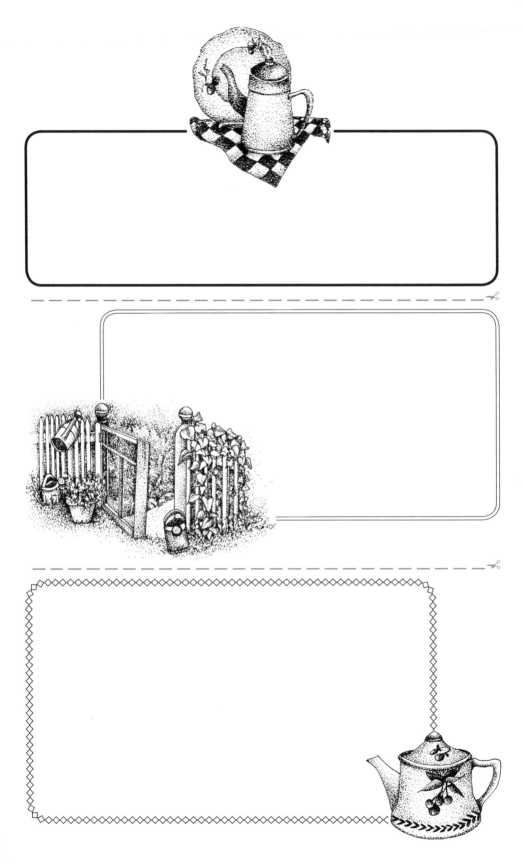

Cherry-Nut Muffins
Instructions for baking:
2 eggs, slightly beaten
$^2/_3$ cup orange juice
$^1/_3$ cup vegetable oil

1. Preheat oven to 375°.
2. Empty contents of jar into large bowl and stir to mix.
3. In separate bowl, whisk eggs, orange juice and vegetable oil and blend well.
4. Add liquid mixture to dry mixture and stir until mixture is just moist.
5. Spoon batter into prepared muffin cups.
6. Bake for 20 minutes or until light brown.

www.cookbookresources.com

- ✄

Cherry-Nut Muffins
Instructions for baking:
2 eggs, slightly beaten
$^2/_3$ cup orange juice
$^1/_3$ cup vegetable oil

1. Preheat oven to 375°.
2. Empty contents of jar into large bowl and stir to mix.
3. In separate bowl, whisk eggs, orange juice and vegetable oil and blend well.
4. Add liquid mixture to dry mixture and stir until mixture is just moist.
5. Spoon batter into prepared muffin cups.
6. Bake for 20 minutes or until light brown.

www.cookbookresources.com

- ✄

Cherry-Nut Muffins
Instructions for baking:
2 eggs, slightly beaten
$^2/_3$ cup orange juice
$^1/_3$ cup vegetable oil

1. Preheat oven to 375°.
2. Empty contents of jar into large bowl and stir to mix.
3. In separate bowl, whisk eggs, orange juice and vegetable oil and blend well.
4. Add liquid mixture to dry mixture and stir until mixture is just moist.
5. Spoon batter into prepared muffin cups.
6. Bake for 20 minutes or until light brown.

Brown Sugar-Pecan Muffins

Brown Sugar-Pecan Muffins

Ingredients for Jar:
2 cups flour
$1/2$ teaspoon salt
$1/2$ teaspoon baking soda
1 teaspoon baking powder
1 cup packed brown sugar
$3/4$ cup coarsely chopped pecans
$1/2$ cup miniature chocolate chips

Instructions for Jar:
1. Combine flour, salt, baking soda and baking powder. Place in bottom of 1-quart jar.

2. Gently spoon brown sugar in even layer over flour mixture.

3. Place pecans over brown sugar.

4. Layer chocolate chips over pecans.

5. Place lid on jar, close and attach baking instructions.

♥ Decorate your jar using the suggestions found on pages 4 and 5.

Brown Sugar-Pecan Muffins

Instructions for baking:

1 egg, slightly beaten
1 cup milk
$^1/_2$ cup (1 stick) butter, melted
$^1/_2$ teaspoon vanilla

1. Preheat oven to 400°.

2. Empty contents of jar into large bowl and stir to mix.

3. In separate bowl, whisk egg, milk, melted butter and vanilla and blend well.

4. Add liquid mixture to dry mixture and stir gently just until mixture is moist.

5. Spoon batter into prepared muffin cups.

6. Bake for 12 to 15 minutes or until brown on top.

" *Life is not measured by the breaths we take but by the moments that take our breath away.*"

~ *Anonymous*

Brown Sugar-Pecan Muffins
Instructions for baking:
1 egg, slightly beaten
1 cup milk
$^1/_2$ cup (1 stick) butter, melted
$^1/_2$ teaspoon vanilla

1. Preheat oven to 400°.
2. Empty contents of jar into large bowl and stir to mix.
3. In separate bowl, whisk egg, milk, melted butter and vanilla and blend well.
4. Add liquid mixture to dry mixture and stir gently just until mixture is moist.
5. Spoon batter into prepared muffin cups.
6. Bake for 12 to 15 minutes or until brown on top.

www.cookbookresources.com

- ✂

Brown Sugar-Pecan Muffins
Instructions for baking:
1 egg, slightly beaten
1 cup milk
$^1/_2$ cup (1 stick) butter, melted
$^1/_2$ teaspoon vanilla

1. Preheat oven to 400°.
2. Empty contents of jar into large bowl and stir to mix.
3. In separate bowl, whisk egg, milk, melted butter and vanilla and blend well.
4. Add liquid mixture to dry mixture and stir gently just until mixture is moist.
5. Spoon batter into prepared muffin cups.
6. Bake for 12 to 15 minutes or until brown on top.

www.cookbookresources.com

- ✂

Brown Sugar-Pecan Muffins
Instructions for baking:
1 egg, slightly beaten
1 cup milk
$^1/_2$ cup (1 stick) butter, melted
$^1/_2$ teaspoon vanilla

1. Preheat oven to 400°.
2. Empty contents of jar into large bowl and stir to mix.
3. In separate bowl, whisk egg, milk, melted butter and vanilla and blend well.
4. Add liquid mixture to dry mixture and stir gently just until mixture is moist.
5. Spoon batter into prepared muffin cups.
6. Bake for 12 to 15 minutes or until brown on top.

www.cookbookresources.com

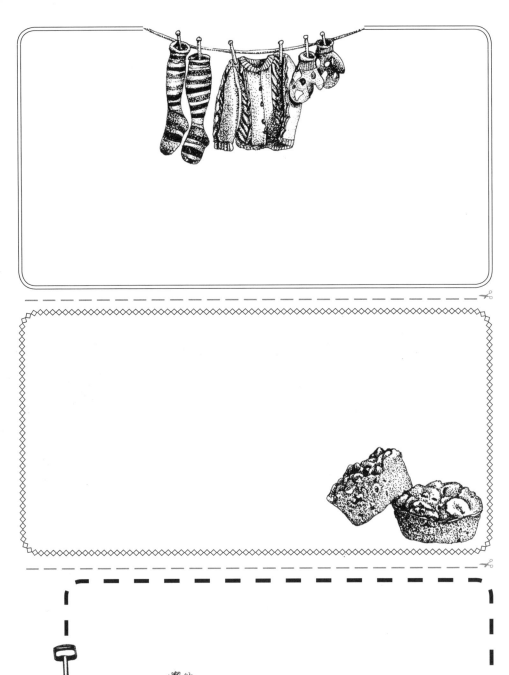

Brown Sugar-Pecan Muffins

Instructions for baking:
1 egg, slightly beaten
1 cup milk
$1/2$ cup (1 stick) butter, melted
$1/2$ teaspoon vanilla

1. Preheat oven to 400°.
2. Empty contents of jar into large bowl and stir to mix.
3. In separate bowl, whisk egg, milk, melted butter and vanilla and blend well.
4. Add liquid mixture to dry mixture and stir gently just until mixture is moist.
5. Spoon batter into prepared muffin cups.
6. Bake for 12 to 15 minutes or until brown on top.

www.cookbookresources.com

Brown Sugar-Pecan Muffins

Instructions for baking:
1 egg, slightly beaten
1 cup milk
$1/2$ cup (1 stick) butter, melted
$1/2$ teaspoon vanilla

1. Preheat oven to 400°.
2. Empty contents of jar into large bowl and stir to mix.
3. In separate bowl, whisk egg, milk, melted butter and vanilla and blend well.
4. Add liquid mixture to dry mixture and stir gently just until mixture is moist.
5. Spoon batter into prepared muffin cups.
6. Bake for 12 to 15 minutes or until brown on top.

www.cookbookresources.com

Brown Sugar-Pecan Muffins

Instructions for baking:
1 egg, slightly beaten
1 cup milk
$1/2$ cup (1 stick) butter, melted
$1/2$ teaspoon vanilla

1. Preheat oven to 400°.
2. Empty contents of jar into large bowl and stir to mix.
3. In separate bowl, whisk egg, milk, melted butter and vanilla and blend well.
4. Add liquid mixture to dry mixture and stir gently just until mixture is moist.
5. Spoon batter into prepared muffin cups.
6. Bake for 12 to 15 minutes or until brown on top.

German Chocolate Muffins

German Chocolate Muffins

Ingredients for Jar:

$1/2$ cup sugar
$1^1/2$ cups flour
$1/2$ cup cocoa powder
1 tablespoon baking powder
$1/4$ teaspoon salt
$1/2$ cup miniature chocolate chips
$1/2$ cup chopped pecans
$1/2$ cup sweetened, shredded coconut

Instructions for Jar:

1. Pour sugar into bottom of 1-quart jar.

2. In separate bowl, combine flour with cocoa powder, baking powder and salt.

3. Spoon flour mixture evenly over sugar.

4. Layer chocolate chips over flour mixture, then top with layer of chopped pecans.

5. Place coconut over pecans.

6. Place lid on jar, close and attach baking instructions.

German Chocolate Muffins

Instructions for baking:

$^1/_4$ cup ($^1/_2$ stick) butter, melted
2 eggs, slightly beaten
$^3/_4$ cup milk
1 teaspoon vanilla

1. Preheat oven to 400°.

2. Empty contents of jar into large bowl and stir to mix.

3. In separate bowl, whisk melted butter, eggs, milk and vanilla.

4. Add liquid mixture to dry mixture and stir just until mixture is moist.

5. Spoon batter into 12 prepared muffin cups.

6. Bake for 18 to 20 minutes or until cake tester comes out clean.

> "*The best portion of a good man's life are
> his little, nameless, unremembered
> acts of kindness and love.*"
> ~*William Wordsworth*

German Chocolate Muffins
Instructions for baking:
$1/4$ cup ($1/2$ stick) butter, melted
2 eggs, slightly beaten
$3/4$ cup milk
1 teaspoon vanilla

1. Preheat oven to 400°.
2. Empty contents of jar into large bowl and stir to mix.
3. In separate bowl, whisk melted butter, eggs, milk and vanilla.
4. Add liquid mixture to dry mixture and stir just until mixture is moist.
5. Spoon batter into 12 prepared muffin cups.
6. Bake for 18 to 20 minutes or until cake tester comes out clean.

www.cookbookresources.com

- -

German Chocolate Muffins
Instructions for baking:
$1/4$ cup ($1/2$ stick) butter, melted
2 eggs, slightly beaten
$3/4$ cup milk
1 teaspoon vanilla

1. Preheat oven to 400°.
2. Empty contents of jar into large bowl and stir to mix.
3. In separate bowl, whisk melted butter, eggs, milk and vanilla.
4. Add liquid mixture to dry mixture and stir just until mixture is moist.
5. Spoon batter into 12 prepared muffin cups.
6. Bake for 18 to 20 minutes or until cake tester comes out clean.

www.cookbookresources.com

- -

German Chocolate Muffins
Instructions for baking:
$1/4$ cup ($1/2$ stick) butter, melted
2 eggs, slightly beaten
$3/4$ cup milk
1 teaspoon vanilla

1. Preheat oven to 400°.
2. Empty contents of jar into large bowl and stir to mix.
3. In separate bowl, whisk melted butter, eggs, milk and vanilla.
4. Add liquid mixture to dry mixture and stir just until mixture is moist.
5. Spoon batter into 12 prepared muffin cups.
6. Bake for 18 to 20 minutes or until cake tester comes out clean.

www.cookbookresources.com

German Chocolate Muffins

Instructions for baking:

$^1/_4$ cup ($^1/_2$ stick) butter, melted
2 eggs, slightly beaten
$^3/_4$ cup milk
1 teaspoon vanilla

1. Preheat oven to 400°.
2. Empty contents of jar into large bowl and stir to mix.
3. In separate bowl, whisk melted butter, eggs, milk and vanilla.
4. Add liquid mixture to dry mixture and stir just until mixture is moist.
5. Spoon batter into 12 prepared muffin cups.
6. Bake for 18 to 20 minutes or until cake tester comes out clean.

www.cookbookresources.com

German Chocolate Muffins

Instructions for baking:

$^1/_4$ cup ($^1/_2$ stick) butter, melted
2 eggs, slightly beaten
$^3/_4$ cup milk
1 teaspoon vanilla

1. Preheat oven to 400°.
2. Empty contents of jar into large bowl and stir to mix.
3. In separate bowl, whisk melted butter, eggs, milk and vanilla.
4. Add liquid mixture to dry mixture and stir just until mixture is moist.
5. Spoon batter into 12 prepared muffin cups.
6. Bake for 18 to 20 minutes or until cake tester comes out clean.

www.cookbookresources.com

German Chocolate Muffins

Instructions for baking:

$^1/_4$ cup ($^1/_2$ stick) butter, melted
2 eggs, slightly beaten
$^3/_4$ cup milk
1 teaspoon vanilla

1. Preheat oven to 400°.
2. Empty contents of jar into large bowl and stir to mix.
3. In separate bowl, whisk melted butter, eggs, milk and vanilla.
4. Add liquid mixture to dry mixture and stir just until mixture is moist.
5. Spoon batter into 12 prepared muffin cups.
6. Bake for 18 to 20 minutes or until cake tester comes out clean.

www.cookbookresources.com

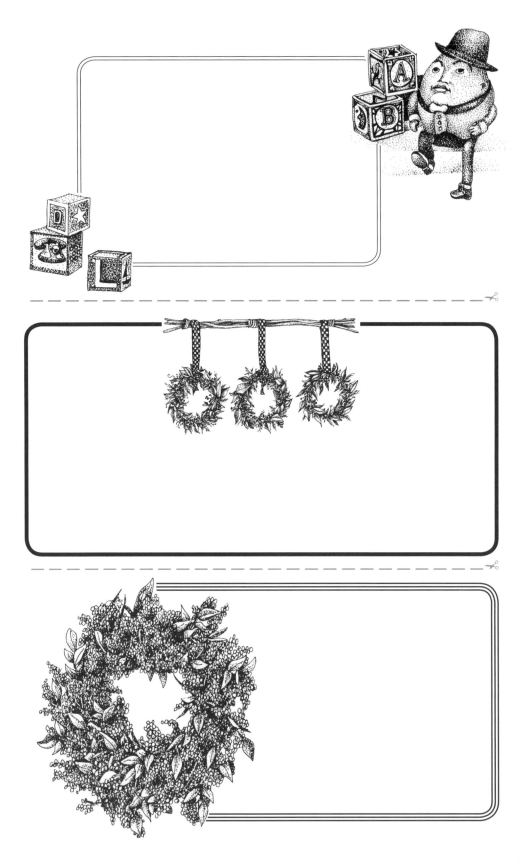

Cherry-Almond Muffins

Cherry-Almond Muffins

Ingredients for Jar:
2 cups flour
1 tablespoon baking powder
$1/4$ teaspoon salt
$1/4$ teaspoon cinnamon
$1/4$ teaspoon grated nutmeg
$1/2$ cup sugar
$1/2$ cup finely chopped almonds
1 cup dried, sweetened cherries

Instructions for Jar:

1. Combine flour with baking powder and salt. Spoon into bottom of 1-quart jar.

2. In small bowl, stir cinnamon and nutmeg thoroughly into sugar. Spoon evenly over flour mixture.

3. Layer almonds over sugar mixture and top with cherries.

5. Place lid on jar, close and attach baking instructions.

Cherry-Almond Muffins

Instructions for baking:

³/₄ cup milk
1 egg, slightly beaten
¹/₃ cup vegetable oil
¹/₂ teaspoon almond extract

1. Preheat oven to 400°.

2. Empty contents of jar into large bowl and stir to mix.

3. In separate bowl, whisk milk, egg, oil and almond extract.

4. Add liquid mixture to dry ingredients and mix just until moist.

5. Spoon batter into 12 prepared muffin cups.

6. Bake for 10 to 15 minutes or until tester comes out clean.

"It has been said that we need just three things in life: Something to do, something to look forward to and someone to love."

~Anonymous

Cherry-Almond Muffins
Instructions for baking:
$3/4$ cup milk
1 egg, slightly beaten
$1/3$ cup vegetable oil
$1/2$ teaspoon almond extract

1. Preheat oven to 400°.
2. Empty contents of jar into large bowl and stir to mix.
3. In separate bowl, whisk milk, egg, oil and almond extract.
4. Add liquid mixture to dry ingredients and mix just until moist.
5. Spoon batter into 12 prepared muffin cups.
6. Bake for 10 to 15 minutes or until tester comes out clean.

Cherry-Almond Muffins
Instructions for baking:
$3/4$ cup milk
1 egg, slightly beaten
$1/3$ cup vegetable oil
$1/2$ teaspoon almond extract

1. Preheat oven to 400°.
2. Empty contents of jar into large bowl and stir to mix.
3. In separate bowl, whisk milk, egg, oil and almond extract.
4. Add liquid mixture to dry ingredients and mix just until moist.
5. Spoon batter into 12 prepared muffin cups.
6. Bake for 10 to 15 minutes or until tester comes out clean.

Cherry-Almond Muffins
Instructions for baking:
$3/4$ cup milk
1 egg, slightly beaten
$1/3$ cup vegetable oil
$1/2$ teaspoon almond extract

1. Preheat oven to 400°.
2. Empty contents of jar into large bowl and stir to mix.
3. In separate bowl, whisk milk, egg, oil and almond extract.
4. Add liquid mixture to dry ingredients and mix just until moist.
5. Spoon batter into 12 prepared muffin cups.
6. Bake for 10 to 15 minutes or until tester comes out clean.

Cherry-Almond Muffins

Instructions for baking:

$^3/_4$ cup milk
1 egg, slightly beaten
$^1/_3$ cup vegetable oil
$^1/_2$ teaspoon almond extract

1. Preheat oven to 400°.
2. Empty contents of jar into large bowl and stir to mix.
3. In separate bowl, whisk milk, egg, oil and almond extract.
4. Add liquid mixture to dry ingredients and mix just until moist.
5. Spoon batter into 12 prepared muffin cups.
6. Bake for 10 to 15 minutes or until tester comes out clean.

www.cookbookresources.com

- ✂

Cherry-Almond Muffins

Instructions for baking:

$^3/_4$ cup milk
1 egg, slightly beaten
$^1/_3$ cup vegetable oil
$^1/_2$ teaspoon almond extract

1. Preheat oven to 400°.
2. Empty contents of jar into large bowl and stir to mix.
3. In separate bowl, whisk milk, egg, oil and almond extract.
4. Add liquid mixture to dry ingredients and mix just until moist.
5. Spoon batter into 12 prepared muffin cups.
6. Bake for 10 to 15 minutes or until tester comes out clean.

www.cookbookresources.com

- ✂

Cherry-Almond Muffins

Instructions for baking:

$^3/_4$ cup milk
1 egg, slightly beaten
$^1/_3$ cup vegetable oil
$^1/_2$ teaspoon almond extract

1. Preheat oven to 400°.
2. Empty contents of jar into large bowl and stir to mix.
3. In separate bowl, whisk milk, egg, oil and almond extract.
4. Add liquid mixture to dry ingredients and mix just until moist.
5. Spoon batter into 12 prepared muffin cups.
6. Bake for 10 to 15 minutes or until tester comes out clean.

Sweet Coconut Muffins

Sweet Coconut Muffins

Ingredients for Jar:
2 cups flour
$2^1/_2$ teaspoons baking powder
$^1/_2$ teaspoon salt
1 cup sugar
$^1/_2$ cup chocolate chips
1 cup sweetened, shredded coconut

Instructions for Jar:
1. Combine flour with baking powder and salt and spoon into bottom of 1-quart jar.

2. Spoon sugar over flour mixture.

3. Spoon chocolate chips evenly over sugar.

4. Place coconut over chocolate chips and press down gently to fit.

5. Place lid on jar, close and attach baking instructions.

♥ Decorate your jar using the suggestions found on pages 4 and 5.

Sweet Coconut Muffins

Instructions for baking:

$1/2$ cup (1 stick) butter, melted
2 eggs, lightly beaten
1 (8 ounce) container plain yogurt

1. Preheat oven to 375°.

2. Empty contents of jar into large bowl and stir to mix.

3. In separate bowl, whisk melted butter, eggs and yogurt and blend well.

4. Add liquid mixture to dry mixture and stir just until moist.

5. Spoon batter into 12 prepared muffin cups.

6. Bake for 18 to 20 minutes or until tester comes out clean.

"A real friend is one who will tell you of your faults and follies in prosperity and assist with his hand and heart in adversity."
~Anonymous

Sweet Coconut Muffins
Instructions for baking:
$^1/_2$ cup (1 stick) butter, melted
2 eggs, lightly beaten
1 (8 ounce) container plain yogurt

1. Preheat oven to 375°.
2. Empty contents of jar into large bowl and stir to mix.
3. In separate bowl, whisk melted butter, eggs and yogurt and blend well.
4. Add liquid mixture to dry mixture and stir just until moist.
5. Spoon batter into 12 prepared muffin cups.
6. Bake for 18 to 20 minutes or until tester comes out clean.

www.cookbookresources.com

- ✂

Sweet Coconut Muffins
Instructions for baking:
$^1/_2$ cup (1 stick) butter, melted
2 eggs, lightly beaten
1 (8 ounce) container plain yogurt

1. Preheat oven to 375°.
2. Empty contents of jar into large bowl and stir to mix.
3. In separate bowl, whisk melted butter, eggs and yogurt and blend well.
4. Add liquid mixture to dry mixture and stir just until moist.
5. Spoon batter into 12 prepared muffin cups.
6. Bake for 18 to 20 minutes or until tester comes out clean.

www.cookbookresources.com

- ✂

Sweet Coconut Muffins
Instructions for baking:
$^1/_2$ cup (1 stick) butter, melted
2 eggs, lightly beaten
1 (8 ounce) container plain yogurt

1. Preheat oven to 375°.
2. Empty contents of jar into large bowl and stir to mix.
3. In separate bowl, whisk melted butter, eggs and yogurt and blend well.
4. Add liquid mixture to dry mixture and stir just until moist.
5. Spoon batter into 12 prepared muffin cups.
6. Bake for 18 to 20 minutes or until tester comes out clean.

www.cookbookresources.com

Sweet Coconut Muffins

Instructions for baking:
$^1/_2$ cup (1 stick) butter, melted
2 eggs, lightly beaten
1 (8 ounce) container plain yogurt

1. Preheat oven to 375°.
2. Empty contents of jar into large bowl and stir to mix.
3. In separate bowl, whisk melted butter, eggs and yogurt and blend well.
4. Add liquid mixture to dry mixture and stir just until moist.
5. Spoon batter into 12 prepared muffin cups.
6. Bake for 18 to 20 minutes or until tester comes out clean.

www.cookbookresources.com

- ✂

Sweet Coconut Muffins

Instructions for baking:
$^1/_2$ cup (1 stick) butter, melted
2 eggs, lightly beaten
1 (8 ounce) container plain yogurt

1. Preheat oven to 375°.
2. Empty contents of jar into large bowl and stir to mix.
3. In separate bowl, whisk melted butter, eggs and yogurt and blend well.
4. Add liquid mixture to dry mixture and stir just until moist.
5. Spoon batter into 12 prepared muffin cups.
6. Bake for 18 to 20 minutes or until tester comes out clean.

www.cookbookresources.com

- ✂

Sweet Coconut Muffins

Instructions for baking:
$^1/_2$ cup (1 stick) butter, melted
2 eggs, lightly beaten
1 (8 ounce) container plain yogurt

1. Preheat oven to 375°.
2. Empty contents of jar into large bowl and stir to mix.
3. In separate bowl, whisk melted butter, eggs and yogurt and blend well.
4. Add liquid mixture to dry mixture and stir just until moist.
5. Spoon batter into 12 prepared muffin cups.
6. Bake for 18 to 20 minutes or until tester comes out clean.

www.cookbookresources.com

Cranberry-Corn Muffins

Cranberry-Corn Muffins

Ingredients for Jar:

1 cup firmly packed light brown sugar
1 cup flour
2 teaspoons baking powder
$2/3$ cup yellow corn meal
$1^1/4$ cups dried, sweetened cranberries

Instructions for Jar:

1. Spoon brown sugar evenly into bottom of 1-quart jar.

2. Combine flour and baking powder and spoon evenly over sugar.

3. Layer corn meal over flour and top with cranberries.

4. Place lid on jar, close and attach baking instructions.

♥ Decorate your jar using the suggestions found on pages 4 and 5.

Cranberry-Corn Muffins

Instructions for baking:

2 eggs, slightly beaten
1/2 cup milk
1/2 cup (1 stick) butter, melted

1. Preheat oven to 375°.

2. Empty contents of jar into large bowl and stir to mix.

3. In separate bowl, whisk eggs, milk and melted butter.

4. Add liquid mixture to dry ingredients and stir just until mixture is moist.

5. Spoon batter into 12 prepared muffin cups.

6. Bake for 18 to 20 minutes or until tester comes out clean.

"*A* smile costs nothing but gives much. It takes but a moment but the memory of it can last forever."
~ *Anonymous*

Cranberry-Corn Muffins
Instructions for baking:
2 eggs, slightly beaten
$1/2$ cup milk
$1/2$ cup (1 stick) butter, melted
1. Preheat oven to 375°.
2. Empty contents of jar into large bowl and stir to mix.
3. In separate bowl, whisk eggs, milk and melted butter.
4. Add liquid mixture to dry ingredients and stir just until mixture is moist.
5. Spoon batter into 12 prepared muffin cups.
6. Bake for 18 to 20 minutes or until tester comes out clean.

Cranberry-Corn Muffins
Instructions for baking:
2 eggs, slightly beaten
$1/2$ cup milk
$1/2$ cup (1 stick) butter, melted

1. Preheat oven to 375°.
2. Empty contents of jar into large bowl and stir to mix.
3. In separate bowl, whisk eggs, milk and melted butter.
4. Add liquid mixture to dry ingredients and stir just until mixture is moist.
5.. Spoon batter into 12 prepared muffin cups.
6. Bake for 18 to 20 minutes or until tester comes out clean.

Cranberry-Corn Muffins
Instructions for baking:
2 eggs, slightly beaten
$1/2$ cup milk
$1/2$ cup (1 stick) butter, melted
1. Preheat oven to 375°.
2. Empty contents of jar into large bowl and stir to mix.
3. In separate bowl, whisk eggs, milk and melted butter.
4. Add liquid mixture to dry ingredients and stir just until mixture is moist.
5. Spoon batter into 12 prepared muffin cups.
6. Bake for 18 to 20 minutes or until tester comes out clean.

Cranberry-Corn Muffins
Instructions for baking:
2 eggs, slightly beaten
1/2 cup milk
1/2 cup (1 stick) butter, melted

1. Preheat oven to 375°.
2. Empty contents of jar into large bowl and stir to mix.
3. In separate bowl, whisk eggs, milk and melted butter.
4. Add liquid mixture to dry ingredients and stir just until mixture is moist.
5. Spoon batter into 12 prepared muffin cups.
6. Bake for 18 to 20 minutes or until tester comes out clean.

Cranberry-Corn Muffins
Instructions for baking:
2 eggs, slightly beaten
1/2 cup milk
1/2 cup (1 stick) butter, melted
1. Preheat oven to 375°.
2. Empty contents of jar into large bowl and stir to mix.
3. In separate bowl, whisk eggs, milk and melted butter.
4. Add liquid mixture to dry ingredients and stir just until mixture is moist.
5. Spoon batter into 12 prepared muffin cups.
6. Bake for 18 to 20 minutes or until tester comes out clean.

Cranberry-Corn Muffins
Instructions for baking:
2 eggs, slightly beaten
1/2 cup milk
1/2 cup (1 stick) butter, melted
1. Preheat oven to 375°.
2. Empty contents of jar into large bowl and stir to mix.
3. In separate bowl, whisk eggs, milk and melted butter.
4. Add liquid mixture to dry ingredients and stir just until mixture is moist.
5. Spoon batter into 12 prepared muffin cups.
6. Bake for 18 to 20 minutes or until tester comes out clean.

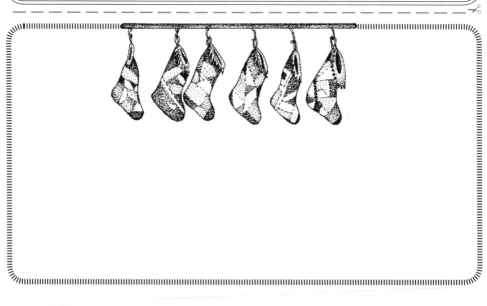

Wholesome Raisin-Spice Muffins

Wholesome Raisin-Spice Muffins

Ingredients for Jar:
2 cups whole wheat flour
1 teaspoon baking soda
2 teaspoons baking powder
$^1/_2$ teaspoon salt
$^3/_4$ cup sugar
1 teaspoon cinnamon
1 cup raisins
$^1/_2$ cup chopped walnuts

Instructions for Jar:
1. Mix flour with baking soda, baking powder and salt. Spoon into bottom of 1-quart jar.

2. In separate bowl, combine sugar with cinnamon and mix thoroughly.

3. Spoon sugar mixture evenly over flour mixture.

4. Layer raisins over sugar mixture and top with walnuts.

5. Place lid on jar, close and attach baking instructions.

♥ Decorate your jar using the suggestions found on pages 4 and 5.

Wholesome Raisin-Spice Muffins

Instructions for baking:

$1/3$ cup ($2/3$ stick) butter, melted
1 egg, slightly beaten
1 (8 ounce) container vanilla yogurt

1. Preheat oven to 350°.

2. Empty contents of jar into large bowl and stir to mix.

3. In separate bowl, whisk melted butter, egg and yogurt and blend well.

4. Add liquid mixture to dry mixture and stir just until mixture is moist.

5. Spoon batter into 12 prepared muffin cups.

6. Bake for 15 minutes or until light brown on top.

"*Treat people as if they were what they ought to be and you help them to become the person they are capable of being.*"

~Goethe

Wholesome Raisin-Spice Muffins
Instructions for baking:
$^1/_3$ cup ($^2/_3$ stick) butter, melted
1 egg, slightly beaten
1 (8 ounce) container vanilla yogurt

1. Preheat oven to 350°.
2. Empty contents of jar into large bowl and stir to mix.
3. In separate bowl, whisk melted butter, egg and yogurt and blend well.
4. Add liquid mixture to dry mixture and stir just until mixture is moist.
5. Spoon batter into 12 prepared muffin cups.
6. Bake for 15 minutes or until light brown on top.

- ✂

Wholesome Raisin-Spice Muffins
Instructions for baking:
$^1/_3$ cup ($^2/_3$ stick) butter, melted
1 egg, slightly beaten
1 (8 ounce) container vanilla yogurt

1. Preheat oven to 350°.
2. Empty contents of jar into large bowl and stir to mix.
3. In separate bowl, whisk melted butter, egg and yogurt and blend well.
4. Add liquid mixture to dry mixture and stir just until mixture is moist.
5. Spoon batter into 12 prepared muffin cups.
6. Bake for 15 minutes or until light brown on top.

- ✂

Wholesome Raisin-Spice Muffins
Instructions for baking:
$^1/_3$ cup ($^2/_3$ stick) butter, melted
1 egg, slightly beaten
1 (8 ounce) container vanilla yogurt

1. Preheat oven to 350°.
2. Empty contents of jar into large bowl and stir to mix.
3. In separate bowl, whisk melted butter, egg and yogurt and blend well.
4. Add liquid mixture to dry mixture and stir just until mixture is moist.
5. Spoon batter into 12 prepared muffin cups.
6. Bake for 15 minutes or until light brown on top.

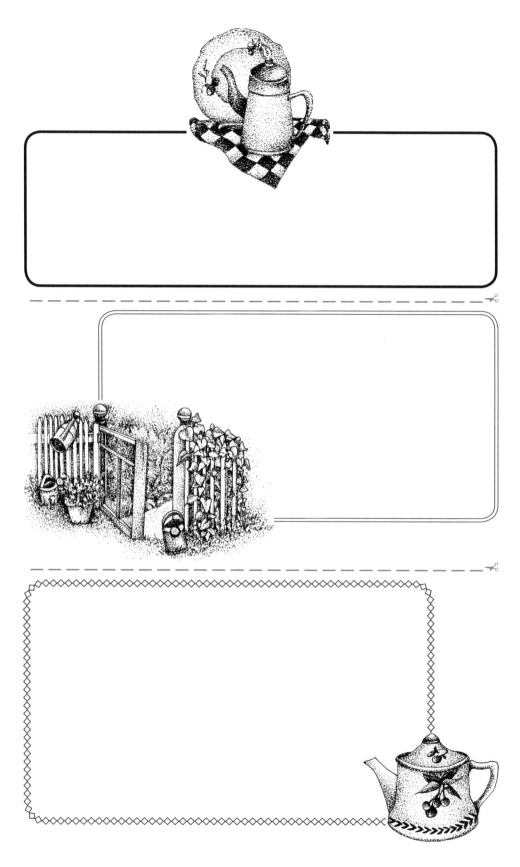

Wholesome Raisin-Spice Muffins

Instructions for baking:

$1/3$ cup ($2/3$ stick) butter, melted
1 egg, slightly beaten
1 (8 ounce) container vanilla yogurt

1. Preheat oven to 350°.
2. Empty contents of jar into large bowl and stir to mix.
3. In separate bowl, whisk melted butter, egg and yogurt and blend well.
4. Add liquid mixture to dry mixture and stir just until mixture is moist.
5. Spoon batter into 12 prepared muffin cups.
6. Bake for 15 minutes or until light brown on top.

Wholesome Raisin-Spice Muffins

Instructions for baking:

$1/3$ cup ($2/3$ stick) butter, melted
1 egg, slightly beaten
1 (8 ounce) container vanilla yogurt

1. Preheat oven to 350°.
2. Empty contents of jar into large bowl and stir to mix.
3. In separate bowl, whisk melted butter, egg and yogurt and blend well.
4. Add liquid mixture to dry mixture and stir just until mixture is moist.
5. Spoon batter into 12 prepared muffin cups.
6. Bake for 15 minutes or until light brown on top.

www.cookbookresources.com

Wholesome Raisin-Spice Muffins

Instructions for baking:

$1/3$ cup ($2/3$ stick) butter, melted
1 egg, slightly beaten
1 (8 ounce) container vanilla yogurt

1. Preheat oven to 350°.
2. Empty contents of jar into large bowl and stir to mix.
3. In separate bowl, whisk melted butter, egg and yogurt and blend well.
4. Add liquid mixture to dry mixture and stir just until mixture is moist.
5. Spoon batter into 12 prepared muffin cups.
6. Bake for 15 minutes or until light brown on top.

Pina Colada Muffins

Pina Colada Muffins

Ingredients for Jar:

2 cups flour
1 tablespoon baking powder
$^1/_2$ teaspoon salt
$^1/_2$ cup sugar
1 cup sweetened, shredded coconut
$^3/_4$ cup chopped macadamia nuts or almonds

Instructions for Jar:

1. Combine flour, baking powder and salt. Spoon into bottom of 1-quart jar.

2. Spoon sugar over flour mixture.

3. Layer coconut over sugar and top with macadamia nuts.

4. Place lid on jar, close and attach baking instructions.

♥ Decorate your jar using the suggestions found on pages 4 and 5.

Pina Colada Muffins

Instructions for baking:

1 egg, slightly beaten
$^1/_4$ cup ($^1/_2$ stick) butter, melted
1 (8 ounce) can crushed pineapple with juice

1. Preheat oven to 350°.

2. Empty contents of jar into large bowl and stir to mix.

3. In separate bowl, whisk egg, melted butter and pineapple with juice and blend well.

4. Add liquid mixture to dry mixture and stir just until mixture is moist.

5. Spoon batter into 12 prepared muffin cups.

6. Bake for 25 to 30 minutes or until tester comes out clean.

" Nothing great was ever achieved without enthusiasm."

~Ralph Waldo Emerson

Pina Colada Muffins
Instructions for baking:
1 egg, slightly beaten
$^1/_4$ cup ($^1/_2$ stick) butter, melted
1 (8 ounce) can crushed pineapple with juice

1. Preheat oven to 350°.
2. Empty contents of jar into large bowl and stir to mix.
3. In separate bowl, whisk egg, melted butter and pineapple with juice and blend well.
4. Add liquid mixture to dry mixture and stir just until mixture is moist.
5. Spoon batter into 12 prepared muffin cups.
6. Bake for 25 to 30 minutes or until tester comes out clean.

Pina Colada Muffins
Instructions for baking:
1 egg, slightly beaten
$^1/_4$ cup ($^1/_2$ stick) butter, melted
1 (8 ounce) can crushed pineapple with juice

1. Preheat oven to 350°.
2. Empty contents of jar into large bowl and stir to mix.
3. In separate bowl, whisk egg, melted butter and pineapple with juice and blend well.
4. Add liquid mixture to dry mixture and stir just until mixture is moist.
5. Spoon batter into 12 prepared muffin cups.
6. Bake for 25 to 30 minutes or until tester comes out clean.

Pina Colada Muffins
Instructions for baking:
1 egg, slightly beaten
$^1/_4$ cup ($^1/_2$ stick) butter, melted
1 (8 ounce) can crushed pineapple with juice

1. Preheat oven to 350°.
2. Empty contents of jar into large bowl and stir to mix.
3. In separate bowl, whisk egg, melted butter and pineapple with juice and blend well.
4. Add liquid mixture to dry mixture and stir just until mixture is moist.
5. Spoon batter into 12 prepared muffin cups.
6. Bake for 25 to 30 minutes or until tester comes out clean.

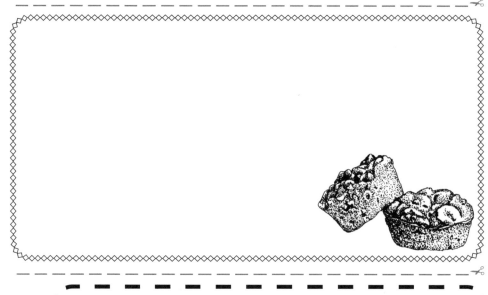

Pina Colada Muffins
Instructions for baking:
1 egg, slightly beaten
$1/4$ cup ($1/2$ stick) butter, melted
1 (8 ounce) can crushed pineapple with juice

1. Preheat oven to 350°.
2. Empty contents of jar into large bowl and stir to mix.
3. In separate bowl, whisk egg, melted butter and pineapple with juice and blend well.
4. Add liquid mixture to dry mixture and stir just until mixture is moist.
5. Spoon batter into 12 prepared muffin cups.
6. Bake for 25 to 30 minutes or until tester comes out clean.

Pina Colada Muffins
Instructions for baking:
1 egg, slightly beaten
$1/4$ cup ($1/2$ stick) butter, melted
1 (8 ounce) can crushed pineapple with juice

1. Preheat oven to 350°.
2. Empty contents of jar into large bowl and stir to mix.
3. In separate bowl, whisk egg, melted butter and pineapple with juice and blend well.
4. Add liquid mixture to dry mixture and stir just until mixture is moist.
5. Spoon batter into 12 prepared muffin cups.
6. Bake for 25 to 30 minutes or until tester comes out clean.

Pina Colada Muffins
Instructions for baking:
1 egg, slightly beaten
$1/4$ cup ($1/2$ stick) butter, melted
1 (8 ounce) can crushed pineapple with juice

1. Preheat oven to 350°.
2. Empty contents of jar into large bowl and stir to mix.
3. In separate bowl, whisk egg, melted butter and pineapple with juice and blend well.
4. Add liquid mixture to dry mixture and stir just until mixture is moist.
5. Spoon batter into 12 prepared muffin cups.
6. Bake for 25 to 30 minutes or until tester comes out clean.

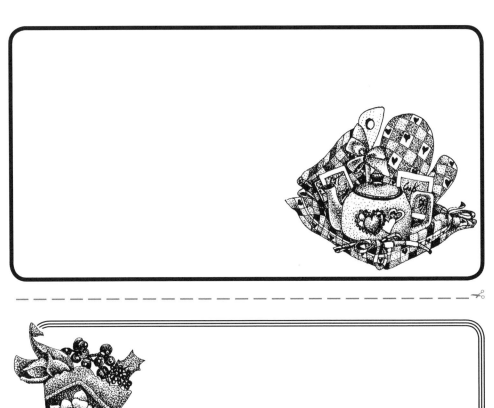

Apple, Raisin and Cinnamon Muffins

Apple, Raisin and Cinnamon Muffins

Ingredients for Jar:

1 cup sugar
1 teaspoon cinnamon
1 1/2 cups flour
1 teaspoon salt
1 teaspoon baking soda
1 cup chopped dried apple
1/2 cup raisins

Instructions for Jar:

1. Combine cinnamon and sugar and mix thoroughly.

2. Spoon sugar mixture into bottom of 1-quart jar.

3. In separate bowl, combine flour with salt and baking soda. Spoon into jar over sugar mixture.

4. Layer chopped apple over flour mixture and top with raisins.

5. Place lid on jar, close and attach baking instructions.

♥ Decorate your jar using the suggestions found on pages 4 and 5.

Apple, Raisin and Cinnamon Muffins

Instructions for baking:

2 eggs, slightly beaten
$3/4$ cup vegetable oil
$1/4$ cup apple juice

1. Preheat oven to 350°.

2. Empty contents of jar into large bowl and stir to mix.

3. In separate bowl, whisk eggs, vegetable oil and apple juice and blend well.

4. Add liquid mixture to dry mixture and stir just until mixture is moist.

5. Spoon batter into 12 prepared muffin pans.

6. Bake for 15 to 20 minutes.

"*Dance like no one is looking and love like you'll never get hurt.*"

~*Anonymous*

Apple, Raisin and Cinnamon Muffins
Instructions for baking:
2 eggs, slightly beaten
$^3/_4$ cup vegetable oil
$^1/_4$ cup apple juice

1. Preheat oven to 350°.
2. Empty contents of jar into large bowl and stir to mix.
3. In separate bowl, whisk eggs, vegetable oil and apple juice and blend well.
4. Add liquid mixture to dry mixture and stir just until mixture is moist.
5. Spoon batter into 12 prepared muffin pans.
6. Bake for 15 to 20 minutes.

www.cookbookresources.com

- ✂

Apple, Raisin and Cinnamon Muffins
Instructions for baking:
2 eggs, slightly beaten
$^3/_4$ cup vegetable oil
$^1/_4$ cup apple juice

1. Preheat oven to 350°.
2. Empty contents of jar into large bowl and stir to mix.
3. In separate bowl, whisk eggs, vegetable oil and apple juice and blend well.
4. Add liquid mixture to dry mixture and stir just until mixture is moist.
5. Spoon batter into 12 prepared muffin pans.
6. Bake for 15 to 20 minutes.

www.cookbookresources.com

- ✂

Apple, Raisin and Cinnamon Muffins
Instructions for baking:
2 eggs, slightly beaten
$^3/_4$ cup vegetable oil
$^1/_4$ cup apple juice

1. Preheat oven to 350°.
2. Empty contents of jar into large bowl and stir to mix.
3. In separate bowl, whisk eggs, vegetable oil and apple juice and blend well.
4. Add liquid mixture to dry mixture and stir just until mixture is moist.
5. Spoon batter into 12 prepared muffin pans.
6. Bake for 15 to 20 minutes.

www.cookbookresources.com

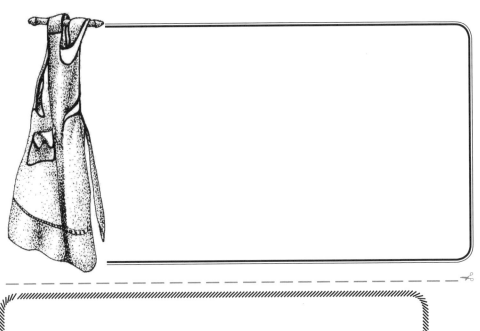

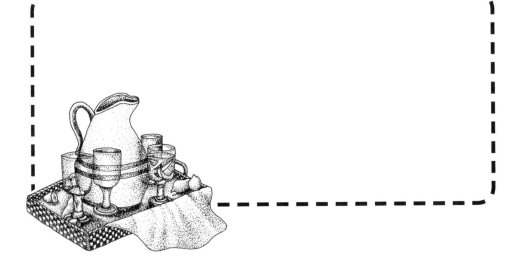

Apple, Raisin and Cinnamon Muffins

Instructions for baking:
2 eggs, slightly beaten
$3/4$ cup vegetable oil
$1/4$ cup apple juice

1. Preheat oven to 350°.
2. Empty contents of jar into large bowl and stir to mix.
3. In separate bowl, whisk eggs, vegetable oil and apple juice and blend well.
4. Add liquid mixture to dry mixture and stir just until mixture is moist.
5. Spoon batter into 12 prepared muffin pans.
6. Bake for 15 to 20 minutes.

www.cookbookresources.com

Apple, Raisin and Cinnamon Muffins

Instructions for baking:
2 eggs, slightly beaten
$3/4$ cup vegetable oil
$1/4$ cup apple juice

1. Preheat oven to 350°.
2. Empty contents of jar into large bowl and stir to mix.
3. In separate bowl, whisk eggs, vegetable oil and apple juice and blend well.
4. Add liquid mixture to dry mixture and stir just until mixture is moist.
5. Spoon batter into 12 prepared muffin pans.
6. Bake for 15 to 20 minutes.

www.cookbookresources.com

Apple, Raisin and Cinnamon Muffins

Instructions for baking:
2 eggs, slightly beaten
$3/4$ cup vegetable oil
$1/4$ cup apple juice

1. Preheat oven to 350°.
2. Empty contents of jar into large bowl and stir to mix.
3. In separate bowl, whisk eggs, vegetable oil and apple juice and blend well.
4. Add liquid mixture to dry mixture and stir just until mixture is moist.
5. Spoon batter into 12 prepared muffin pans.
6. Bake for 15 to 20 minutes.

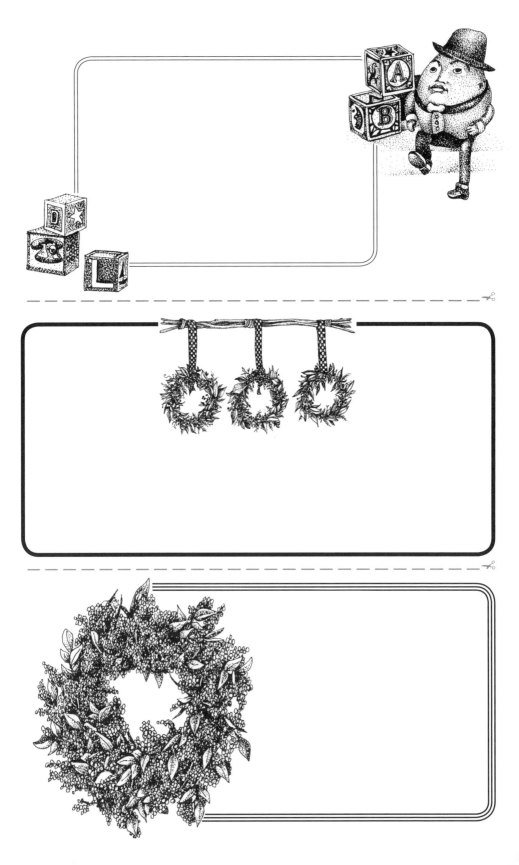

Chocolate-Cherry Muffins

Chocolate-Cherry Muffins

Ingredients for Jar:
2 cups flour
1 tablespoon baking powder
1 teaspoon salt
$1/2$ cup sugar
$1/3$ cup packed brown sugar
1 cup chocolate chips
$1/2$ cup dried, sweetened cherries

Instructions for Jar:

1. Combine flour with baking powder and salt. Spoon into bottom of 1-quart jar.

2. Spoon sugar evenly over flour mixture.

3. Gently spoon brown sugar in even layer over sugar.

4. Layer chocolate chips over brown sugar.

5. Place cherries over chocolate chips (you may have to press down gently to fit).

6. Place lid on jar, close and attach baking instructions.

Chocolate-Cherry Muffins

Instructions for baking:

1 egg, slightly beaten
$^{1}/_{2}$ cup (1 stick) butter, melted
$^{1}/_{2}$ cup milk
$^{1}/_{2}$ cup vanilla yogurt

1. Preheat oven to 350°.

2. Empty contents of jar into large bowl and stir to mix.

3. In separate bowl, whisk eggs, melted butter, milk and yogurt and blend well.

4. Add liquid mixture into dry mixture and stir just until moist.

5. Spoon batter into 12 prepared muffin cups.

6. Bake for 15 to 18 minutes or until tester comes out clean.

"We cannot really love anybody with whom we never laugh."

~Agnes Repplier

Chocolate-Cherry Muffins
Instructions for baking:
1 egg, slightly beaten
$1/2$ cup (1 stick) butter, melted
$1/2$ cup milk
$1/2$ cup vanilla yogurt

1. Preheat oven to 350°.
2. Empty contents of jar into large bowl and stir to mix.
3. In separate bowl, whisk eggs, melted butter, milk and yogurt and blend well.
4. Add liquid mixture into dry mixture and stir just until moist.
5. Spoon batter into 12 prepared muffin cups.
6. Bake for 15 to 18 minutes or until tester comes out clean.

- ✂

Chocolate-Cherry Muffins
Instructions for baking:
1 egg, slightly beaten
$1/2$ cup (1 stick) butter, melted
$1/2$ cup milk
$1/2$ cup vanilla yogurt

1. Preheat oven to 350°.
2. Empty contents of jar into large bowl and stir to mix.
3. In separate bowl, whisk eggs, melted butter, milk and yogurt and blend well.
4. Add liquid mixture into dry mixture and stir just until moist.
5. Spoon batter into 12 prepared muffin cups.
6. Bake for 15 to 18 minutes or until tester comes out clean.

- ✂

Chocolate-Cherry Muffins
Instructions for baking:
1 egg, slightly beaten
$1/2$ cup (1 stick) butter, melted
$1/2$ cup milk
$1/2$ cup vanilla yogurt

1. Preheat oven to 350°.
2. Empty contents of jar into large bowl and stir to mix.
3. In separate bowl, whisk eggs, melted butter, milk and yogurt and blend well.
4. Add liquid mixture into dry mixture and stir just until moist.
5. Spoon batter into 12 prepared muffin cups.
6. Bake for 15 to 18 minutes or until tester comes out clean.

Chocolate-Cherry Muffins

Instructions for baking:

1 egg, slightly beaten
$^1/_2$ cup (1 stick) butter, melted
$^1/_2$ cup milk
$^1/_2$ cup vanilla yogurt

1. Preheat oven to 350°.
2. Empty contents of jar into large bowl and stir to mix.
3. In separate bowl, whisk eggs, melted butter, milk and yogurt and blend well.
4. Add liquid mixture into dry mixture and stir just until moist.
5. Spoon batter into 12 prepared muffin cups.
6. Bake for 15 to 18 minutes or until tester comes out clean.

www.cookbookresources.com

Chocolate-Cherry Muffins

Instructions for baking:

1 egg, slightly beaten
$^1/_2$ cup (1 stick) butter, melted
$^1/_2$ cup milk
$^1/_2$ cup vanilla yogurt

1. Preheat oven to 350°.
2. Empty contents of jar into large bowl and stir to mix.
3. In separate bowl, whisk eggs, melted butter, milk and yogurt and blend well.
4. Add liquid mixture into dry mixture and stir just until moist.
5. Spoon batter into 12 prepared muffin cups.
6. Bake for 15 to 18 minutes or until tester comes out clean.

www.cookbookresources.com

Chocolate-Cherry Muffins

Instructions for baking:

1 egg, slightly beaten
$^1/_2$ cup (1 stick) butter, melted
$^1/_2$ cup milk
$^1/_2$ cup vanilla yogurt

1. Preheat oven to 350°.
2. Empty contents of jar into large bowl and stir to mix.
3. In separate bowl, whisk eggs, melted butter, milk and yogurt and blend well.
4. Add liquid mixture into dry mixture and stir just until moist.
5. Spoon batter into 12 prepared muffin cups.
6. Bake for 15 to 18 minutes or until tester comes out clean.

Airy Parmesan-Herb Muffins

Airy Parmesan-Herb Muffins

Ingredients for Jar:
3 cups flour
2 tablespoons sugar
2 teaspoons baking powder
1 teaspoon salt
1 teaspoon baking soda
1 teaspoon sage
$1/2$ cup dried parsley
$1/2$ cup grated parmesan cheese

Instructions for Jar:

1. Combine all dry ingredients. Mix thoroughly.

2. Spoon into 1-quart jar.

3. Place lid on jar, close and attach baking instructions.

♥ Decorate your jar using the suggestions found
   on pages 4 and 5.

Airy Parmesan-Herb Muffins

Instructions for baking:

2¹/₂ cups buttermilk
¹/₂ cup (1 stick) butter, melted
2 eggs, slightly beaten

1. Preheat oven to 400°.

2. Empty contents of jar into large bowl and stir to mix.

3. In separate bowl, whisk buttermilk, melted butter and eggs and blend well.

4. Add liquid mixture to dry mixture and stir gently just until mixture is moist.

5. Spoon batter into prepared muffin cups.

6. Bake for 15 to 20 minutes or until light brown.

Note: This recipe makes 24 muffins. If you want to make 12 muffins now and 12 later, cut the ingredients in half.

Tip: To make buttermilk, mix 1 cup milk and 1 tablespoon lemon juice or vinegar and set aside for about 10 minutes.

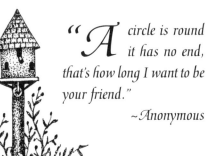

"*A circle is round it has no end, that's how long I want to be your friend.*"

~*Anonymous*

Airy Parmesan-Herb Muffins

Instructions for baking:

2$^{1}/_{2}$ cups buttermilk
$^{1}/_{2}$ cup (1 stick) butter, melted
2 eggs, slightly beaten

1. Preheat oven to 400°.
2. Empty contents of jar into large bowl and stir to mix.
3. In separate bowl, whisk buttermilk, melted butter and eggs and blend well.
4. Add liquid mixture to dry mixture and stir genlly just until mixture is moist.
5. Spoon batter into prepared muffin cups.
6. Bake for 15 to 20 minutes or until light brown.

Note: This recipe makes 24 muffins. If you want to make 12 muffins now and 12 later, cut the ingredients in half.

Tip: To make buttermilk, mix 1 cup milk and 1 tablespoon lemon juice or vinegar and set aside for about 10 minutes.

www.cookbookresources.com

Airy Parmesan-Herb Muffins

Instructions for baking:

2$^{1}/_{2}$ cups buttermilk
$^{1}/_{2}$ cup (1 stick) butter, melted
2 eggs, slightly beaten

1. Preheat oven to 400°.
2. Empty contents of jar into large bowl and stir to mix.
3. In separate bowl, whisk buttermilk, melted butter and eggs and blend well.
4. Add liquid mixture to dry mixture and stir gently just until mixture is moist.
5. Spoon batter into prepared muffin cups.
6. Bake for 15 to 20 minutes or until light brown.

Note: This recipe makes 24 muffins. If you want to make 12 muffins now and 12 later, cut the ingredients in half.

Tip: To make buttermilk, mix 1 cup milk and 1 tablespoon lemon juice or vinegar and set aside for about 10 minutes.

www.cookbookresources.com

Airy Parmesan-Herb Muffins

Instructions for baking:

2$^{1}/_{2}$ cups buttermilk
$^{1}/_{2}$ cup (1 stick) butter, melted
2 eggs, slightly beaten

1. Preheat oven to 400°.
2. Empty contents of jar into large bowl and stir to mix.
3. In separate bowl, whisk buttermilk, melted butter and eggs and blend well.
4. Add liquid mixture to dry mixture and stir gently just until mixture is moist.
5. Spoon batter into prepared muffin cups.
6. Bake for 15 to 20 minutes or until light brown.

Note: This recipe makes 24 muffins. If you want to make 12 muffins now and 12 later, cut the ingredients in half.

Tip: To make buttermilk, mix 1 cup milk and 1 tablespoon lemon juice or vinegar and set aside for about 10 minutes.

www.cookbookresources.com

Airy Parmesan-Herb Muffins
Instructions for baking:
2¹/₂ cups buttermilk
¹/₂ cup (1 stick) butter, melted
2 eggs, slightly beaten

1. Preheat oven to 400°.
2. Empty contents of jar into large bowl and stir to mix.
3. In separate bowl, whisk buttermilk, melted butter and eggs and blend well.
4. Add liquid mixture to dry mixture and stir gently just until mixture is moist.
5. Spoon batter into prepared muffin cups.
6. Bake for 15 to 20 minutes or until light brown.
Note: This recipe makes 24 muffins. If you want to make 12 muffins now and 12 later, cut the ingredients in half.
Tip: To make buttermilk, mix 1 cup milk and 1 tablespoon lemon juice or vinegar and set aside for about 10 minutes.

www.cookbookresources.com

Airy Parmesan-Herb Muffins
Instructions for baking:
2¹/₂ cups buttermilk
¹/₂ cup (1 stick) butter, melted
2 eggs, slightly beaten

1. Preheat oven to 400°.
2. Empty contents of jar into large bowl and stir to mix.
3. In separate bowl, whisk buttermilk, melted butter and eggs and blend well.
4. Add liquid mixture to dry mixture and stir gently just until mixture is moist.
5. Spoon batter into prepared muffin cups.
6. Bake for 15 to 20 minutes or until light brown.
Note: This recipe makes 24 muffins. If you want to make 12 muffins now and 12 later, cut the ingredients in half.
Tip: To make buttermilk, mix 1 cup milk and 1 tablespoon lemon juice or vinegar and set aside for about 10 minutes.

www.cookbookresources.com

Airy Parmesan-Herb Muffins
Instructions for baking:
2¹/₂ cups buttermilk
¹/₂ cup (1 stick) butter, melted
2 eggs, slightly beaten

1. Preheat oven to 400°.
2. Empty contents of jar into large bowl and stir to mix.
3. In separate bowl, whisk buttermilk, melted butter and eggs and blend well.
4. Add liquid mixture to dry mixture and stir gently just until mixture is moist.
5. Spoon batter into prepared muffin cups.
6. Bake for 15 to 20 minutes or until light brown.
Note: This recipe makes 24 muffins. If you want to make 12 muffins now and 12 later, cut the ingredients in half.
Tip: To make buttermilk, mix 1 cup milk and 1 tablespoon lemon juice or vinegar and set aside for about 10 minutes.

www.cookbookresources.com

Chocolate Muffins to the Max

Chocolate Muffins to the Max

Ingredients for Jar:
$1/2$ cup sugar
$1^1/2$ cups flour
$1/2$ cup cocoa powder
1 tablespoon baking powder
$1/4$ teaspoon salt
$1^1/2$ cups miniature chocolate chips

Instructions for Jar:

1. Pour sugar into bottom of 1-quart jar and stir to level.

2. In separate bowl, combine flour with cocoa powder, baking powder and salt.

3. Spoon flour mixture evenly over sugar.

4. Spoon chocolate chips over flour mixture.

5. Place lid on jar, close and attach baking instructions.

♥ Decorate your jar using the suggestions found on pages 4 and 5.

Chocolate Muffins to the Max

Instructions for baking:

¹/₄ cup (¹/₂ stick) butter, melted
2 eggs, slightly beaten
³/₄ cup milk
1 teaspoon vanilla

1. Preheat oven to 400°.

2. Empty contents of jar in large bowl and stir to mix.

3. In separate bowl, whisk melted butter, eggs, milk and vanilla and blend well.

4. Add liquid mixture to dry mixture and stir just until mixture is moist.

5. Spoon batter into 12 prepared muffin cups.

6. Bake for 18 to 20 minutes or until cake tester comes out clean.

"*The future belongs to those who believe in the beauty of their dreams.*"

~Eleanor Roosevelt

Chocolate Muffins to the Max
Instructions for baking:
$^1/_4$ cup ($^1/_2$ stick) butter, melted
2 eggs, slightly beaten
$^3/_4$ cup milk
1 teaspoon vanilla

1. Preheat oven to 400°.
2. Empty contents of jar in large bowl and stir to mix.
3. In separate bowl, whisk melted butter, eggs, milk and vanilla and blend well.
4. Add liquid mixture to dry mixture and stir just until mixture is moist.
5. Spoon batter into 12 prepared muffin cups.
6. Bake for 18 to 20 minutes or until cake tester comes out clean.

www.cookbookresources.com

Chocolate Muffins to the Max
Instructions for baking:
$^1/_4$ cup ($^1/_2$ stick) butter, melted
2 eggs, slightly beaten
$^3/_4$ cup milk
1 teaspoon vanilla

1. Preheat oven to 400°.
2. Empty contents of jar in large bowl and stir to mix.
3. In separate bowl, whisk melted butter, eggs, milk and vanilla and blend well.
4. Add liquid mixture to dry mixture and stir just until mixture is moist.
5. Spoon batter into 12 prepared muffin cups.
6. Bake for 18 to 20 minutes or until cake tester comes out clean.

www.cookbookresources.com

Chocolate Muffins to the Max
Instructions for baking:
$^1/_4$ cup ($^1/_2$ stick) butter, melted
2 eggs, slightly beaten
$^3/_4$ cup milk
1 teaspoon vanilla

1. Preheat oven to 400°.
2. Empty contents of jar in large bowl and stir to mix.
3. In separate bowl, whisk melted butter, eggs, milk and vanilla and blend well.
4. Add liquid mixture to dry mixture and stir just until mixture is moist.
5. Spoon batter into 12 prepared muffin cups.
6. Bake for 18 to 20 minutes or until cake tester comes out clean.

www.cookbookresources.com

Chocolate Muffins to the Max

Instructions for baking:
$^1/_4$ cup ($^1/_2$ stick) butter, melted
2 eggs, slightly beaten
$^3/_4$ cup milk
1 teaspoon vanilla

1. Preheat oven to 400°.
2. Empty contents of jar in large bowl and stir to mix.
3. In separate bowl, whisk melted butter, eggs, milk and vanilla and blend well.
4. Add liquid mixture to dry mixture and stir just until mixture is moist.
5. Spoon batter into 12 prepared muffin cups.
6. Bake for 18 to 20 minutes or until cake tester comes out clean.

Chocolate Muffins to the Max

Instructions for baking:
$^1/_4$ cup ($^1/_2$ stick) butter, melted
2 eggs, slightly beaten
$^3/_4$ cup milk
1 teaspoon vanilla

1. Preheat oven to 400°.
2. Empty contents of jar in large bowl and stir to mix.
3. In separate bowl, whisk melted butter, eggs, milk and vanilla and blend well.
4. Add liquid mixture to dry mixture and stir just until mixture is moist.
5. Spoon batter into 12 prepared muffin cups.
6. Bake for 18 to 20 minutes or until cake tester comes out clean.

Chocolate Muffins to the Max

Instructions for baking:
$^1/_4$ cup ($^1/_2$ stick) butter, melted
2 eggs, slightly beaten
$^3/_4$ cup milk
1 teaspoon vanilla

1. Preheat oven to 400°.
2. Empty contents of jar in large bowl and stir to mix.
3. In separate bowl, whisk melted butter, eggs, milk and vanilla and blend well.
4. Add liquid mixture to dry mixture and stir just until mixture is moist.
5. Spoon batter into 12 prepared muffin cups.
6. Bake for 18 to 20 minutes or until cake tester comes out clean.

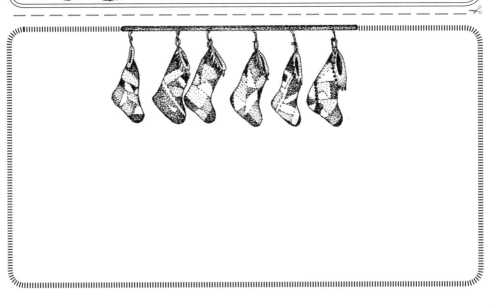

Peanut-Butter Chocolate Muffins

Peanut-Butter Chocolate Muffins

Ingredients for Jar:
$1/2$ cup packed brown sugar
$2^{1}/_{4}$ cups flour
$1/2$ teaspoon salt
1 tablespoon baking powder
$3/_{4}$ cup chocolate chips
$3/_{4}$ cup peanut butter chips

Instructions for Jar:

1. Spoon brown sugar into bottom of 1-quart jar.

2. Mix flour with salt and baking powder. Spoon over
   brown sugar.

3. Place chocolate chips over flour mixture.

4. Place peanut butter chips over chocolate.

5. Place lid on jar, close and attach baking instructions.

♥ Decorate your jar using the suggestions found
   on pages 4 and 5.

Peanut-Butter Chocolate Muffins

Instructions for baking:

$^{2}/_{3}$ cup milk
1 teaspoon vanilla
2 large eggs, slightly beaten
$^{1}/_{2}$ cup (1 stick) butter, melted

1. Preheat oven to 400°.

2. Empty contents of jar into large bowl and stir to mix.

3. In separate bowl, whisk milk, vanilla, eggs and melted butter and blend well.

4. Add liquid mixture to dry mixture and stir just until mixture is moist.

5. Spoon batter into 12 prepared muffin cups.

6. Bake for 15 to 20 minutes.

*"Remember, we all stumble,
every one of us. That's why
it's a comfort to go hand-in-hand."*
~Anonymous

Peanut-Butter Chocolate Muffins

Instructions for baking:

$^2/_3$ cup milk
1 teaspoon vanilla
2 large eggs, slightly beaten
$^1/_2$ cup (1 stick) butter, melted

1. Preheat oven to 400°.
2. Empty contents of jar into large bowl and stir to mix.
3. In separate bowl, whisk milk, vanilla, eggs and melted butter and blend well.
4. Add liquid mixture to dry mixture and stir just until mixture is moist.
5. Spoon batter into 12 prepared muffin cups.
6. Bake for 15 to 20 minutes.

www.cookbookresources.com

Peanut-Butter Chocolate Muffins

Instructions for baking:

$^2/_3$ cup milk
1 teaspoon vanilla
2 large eggs, slightly beaten
$^1/_2$ cup (1 stick) butter, melted

1. Preheat oven to 400°.
2. Empty contents of jar into large bowl and stir to mix.
3. In separate bowl, whisk milk, vanilla, eggs and melted butter and blend well.
4. Add liquid mixture to dry mixture and stir just until mixture is moist.
5. Spoon batter into 12 prepared muffin cups.
6. Bake for 15 to 20 minutes.

www.cookbookresources.com

Peanut-Butter Chocolate Muffins

Instructions for baking:

$^2/_3$ cup milk
1 teaspoon vanilla
2 large eggs, slightly beaten
$^1/_2$ cup (1 stick) butter, melted

1. Preheat oven to 400°.
2. Empty contents of jar into large bowl and stir to mix.
3. In separate bowl, whisk milk, vanilla, eggs and melted butter and blend well.
4. Add liquid mixture to dry mixture and stir just until mixture is moist.
5. Spoon batter into 12 prepared muffin cups.
6. Bake for 15 to 20 minutes.

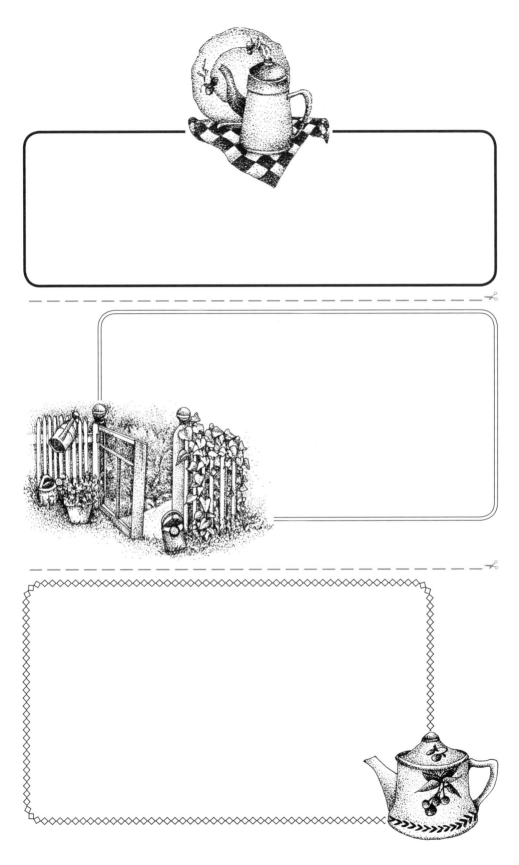

Peanut-Butter Chocolate Muffins
Instructions for baking:
$2/3$ cup milk
1 teaspoon vanilla
2 large eggs, slightly beaten
$1/2$ cup (1 stick) butter, melted

1. Preheat oven to 400°.
2. Empty contents of jar into large bowl and stir to mix.
3. In separate bowl, whisk milk, vanilla, eggs and melted butter and blend well.
4. Add liquid mixture to dry mixture and stir just until mixture is moist.
5. Spoon batter into 12 prepared muffin cups.
6. Bake for 15 to 20 minutes.

- ✂

Peanut-Butter Chocolate Muffins
Instructions for baking:
$2/3$ cup milk
1 teaspoon vanilla
2 large eggs, slightly beaten
$1/2$ cup (1 stick) butter, melted

1. Preheat oven to 400°.
2. Empty contents of jar into large bowl and stir to mix.
3. In separate bowl, whisk milk, vanilla, eggs and melted butter and blend well.
4. Add liquid mixture to dry mixture and stir just until mixture is moist.
5. Spoon batter into 12 prepared muffin cups.
6. Bake for 15 to 20 minutes.

www.cookbookresources.com

- ✂

Peanut-Butter Chocolate Muffins
Instructions for baking:
$2/3$ cup milk
1 teaspoon vanilla
2 large eggs, slightly beaten
$1/2$ cup (1 stick) butter, melted

1. Preheat oven to 400°.
2. Empty contents of jar into large bowl and stir to mix.
3. In separate bowl, whisk milk, vanilla, eggs and melted butter and blend well.
4. Add liquid mixture to dry mixture and stir just until mixture is moist.
5. Spoon batter into 12 prepared muffin cups.
6. Bake for 15 to 20 minutes.

Oat-Apricot Muffins

Oat-Apricot Muffins

Ingredients for Jar:
2 cups flour
3 teaspoons baking powder
1 teaspoon salt
$1/2$ cup sugar
2 teaspoons pumpkin pie spice
$1/2$ cup quick-cooking oats
$3/4$ cup chopped dried apricots
$1/2$ cup chopped nuts

Instructions for Jar:

1. Combine flour, baking powder and salt. Place in bottom of 1-quart jar.

2. Combine sugar and pumpkin pie spice and stir until they mix well. Gently spoon evenly over flour mixture.

3. Spoon oats evenly over sugar mixture.

4. Place apricots over oats.

5. Place nuts over apricots and press down gently if necessary to fit.

6. Place lid on jar, close and attach baking instructions.

Oat-Apricot Muffins

Instructions for baking:

2 eggs, slightly beaten
1 ¹/₃ cups milk
¹/₄ cup vegetable oil

1. Preheat oven to 350°.

2. Empty contents of jar into large bowl and stir to mix.

3. In separate bowl, whisk eggs, milk and vegetable oil and blend well.

4. Add liquid mixture to dry mixture and stir until just moist.

5. Spoon batter into 12 prepared muffin cups.

6. Bake for 30 minutes or until golden brown.

"By the time you are old enough to know that your parents were right, you have children of your own that think you are wrong."

~Anonymous

Oat-Apricot Muffins
Instructions for baking:
2 eggs, slightly beaten
1 $1/_3$ cups milk
$1/_4$ cup vegetable oil

1. Preheat oven to 350°.
2. Empty contents of jar into large bowl and stir to mix.
3. In separate bowl, whisk eggs, milk and vegetable oil and blend well.
4. Add liquid mixture to dry mixture and stir until just moist.
5. Spoon batter into 12 prepared muffin cups.
6. Bake for 30 minutes or until golden brown.

www.cookbookresources.com

- -

Oat-Apricot Muffins
Instructions for baking:
2 eggs, slightly beaten
1 $1/_3$ cups milk
$1/_4$ cup vegetable oil

1. Preheat oven to 350°.
2. Empty contents of jar into large bowl and stir to mix.
3. In separate bowl, whisk eggs, milk and vegetable oil and blend well.
4. Add liquid mixture to dry mixture and stir until just moist.
5. Spoon batter into 12 prepared muffin cups.
6. Bake for 30 minutes or until golden brown.

www.cookbookresources.com

- -

Oat-Apricot Muffins
Instructions for baking:
2 eggs, slightly beaten
1 $1/_3$ cups milk
$1/_4$ cup vegetable oil

1. Preheat oven to 350°.
2. Empty contents of jar into large bowl and stir to mix.
3. In separate bowl, whisk eggs, milk and vegetable oil and blend well.
4. Add liquid mixture to dry mixture and stir until just moist.
5. Spoon batter into 12 prepared muffin cups.
6. Bake for 30 minutes or until golden brown.

Oat-Apricot Muffins
Instructions for baking:
2 eggs, slightly beaten
1 $\frac{1}{3}$ cups milk
$\frac{1}{4}$ cup vegetable oil

1. Preheat oven to 350°.
2. Empty contents of jar into large bowl and stir to mix.
3. In separate bowl, whisk eggs, milk and vegetable oil and blend well.
4. Add liquid mixture to dry mixture and stir until just moist.
5. Spoon batter into 12 prepared muffin cups.
6. Bake for 30 minutes or until golden brown.

www.cookbookresources.com

Oat-Apricot Muffins
Instructions for baking:
2 eggs, slightly beaten
1 $\frac{1}{3}$ cups milk
$\frac{1}{4}$ cup vegetable oil

1. Preheat oven to 350°.
2. Empty contents of jar into large bowl and stir to mix.
3. In separate bowl, whisk eggs, milk and vegetable oil and blend well.
4. Add liquid mixture to dry mixture and stir until just moist.
5. Spoon batter into 12 prepared muffin cups.
6. Bake for 30 minutes or until golden brown.

www.cookbookresources.com

Oat-Apricot Muffins
Instructions for baking:
2 eggs, slightly beaten
1 $\frac{1}{3}$ cups milk
$\frac{1}{4}$ cup vegetable oil

1. Preheat oven to 350°.
2. Empty contents of jar into large bowl and stir to mix.
3. In separate bowl, whisk eggs, milk and vegetable oil and blend well.
4. Add liquid mixture to dry mixture and stir until just moist.
5. Spoon batter into 12 prepared muffin cups.
6. Bake for 30 minutes or until golden brown.

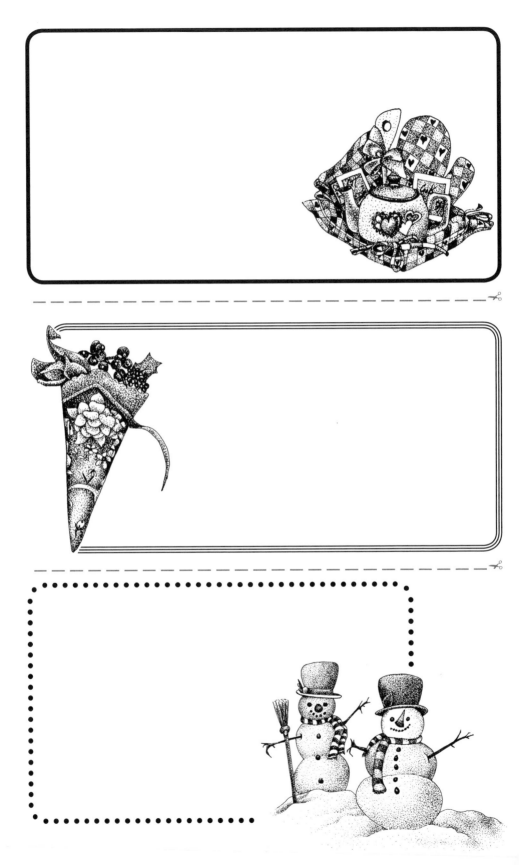

Date-Pineapple Bran Muffins

Date-Pineapple Bran Muffins

Ingredients for Jar:
1¹/₄ cups flour
1 tablespoon baking powder
¹/₂ teaspoon salt
¹/₂ cup packed brown sugar
¹/₂ cup chopped dates
2 cups bran cereal

Instructions for Jar:

1. Combine flour with baking powder and salt and place in bottom of 1-quart jar.

2. Spoon brown sugar evenly over flour mixture.

3. Layer dates over brown sugar and top with bran cereal.

4. Place lid on jar, close and attach baking ingredients.

♥ Decorate your jar using the suggestions found on pages 4 and 5.

Date-Pineapple Bran Muffins

Instructions for baking:

1 egg, slightly beaten
$^1/_4$ cup vegetable oil
$^1/_3$ cup milk
1 (8 ounce) can crushed pineapple with juice

1. Preheat oven to 400°.

2. Empty contents of jar into large bowl and stir to mix.

3. In separate bowl, combine egg, vegetable oil, milk and pineapple with juice and blend well.

4. Add liquid mixture to dry mixture and set aside for 5 minutes to soften bran.

5. Continue stirring just until mixture blends.

6. Spoon batter into 12 prepared muffin cups.

7. Bake for 20 minutes or until tester comes out clean.

" A part of you has grown in me. And so you see, it's you and me together forever, apart maybe in distance, but never in heart."

~Anonymous

Date-Pineapple Bran Muffins

Instructions for baking:
1 egg, slightly beaten
$1/4$ cup vegetable oil
$1/3$ cup milk
1 (8 ounce) can crushed pineapple with juice

1. Preheat oven to 400°.
2. Empty contents of jar into large bowl and stir to mix.
3. In separate bowl, combine egg, vegetable oil, milk and pineapple with juice and blend well.
4. Add liquid mixture to dry mixture and set aside for 5 minutes to soften bran.
5. Continue stirring just until mixture blends.
6. Spoon batter into 12 prepared muffin cups.
7. Bake for 20 minutes or until tester comes out clean.

www.cookbookresources.com

Date-Pineapple Bran Muffins

Instructions for baking:
1 egg, slightly beaten
$1/4$ cup vegetable oil
$1/3$ cup milk
1 (8 ounce) can crushed pineapple with juice

1. Preheat oven to 400°.
2. Empty contents of jar into large bowl and stir to mix.
3. In separate bowl, combine egg, vegetable oil, milk and pineapple with juice and blend well.
4. Add liquid mixture to dry mixture and set aside for 5 minutes to soften bran.
5. Continue stirring just until mixture blends.
6. Spoon batter into 12 prepared muffin cups.
7. Bake for 20 minutes or until tester comes out clean.

www.cookbookresources.com

Date-Pineapple Bran Muffins

Instructions for baking:
1 egg, slightly beaten
$1/4$ cup vegetable oil
$1/3$ cup milk
1 (8 ounce) can crushed pineapple with juice

1. Preheat oven to 400°.
2. Empty contents of jar into large bowl and stir to mix.
3. In separate bowl, combine egg, vegetable oil, milk and pineapple with juice and blend well.
4. Add liquid mixture to dry mixture and set aside for 5 minutes to soften bran.
5. Continue stirring just until mixture blends.
6. Spoon batter into 12 prepared muffin cups.
7. Bake for 20 minutes or until tester comes out clean.

www.cookbookresources.com

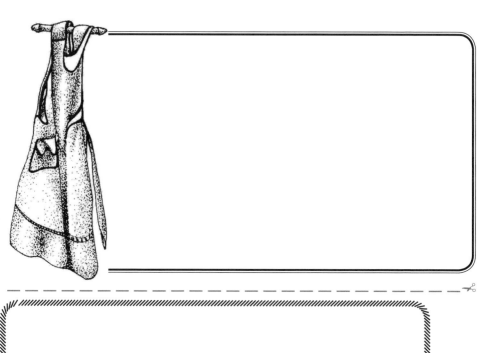

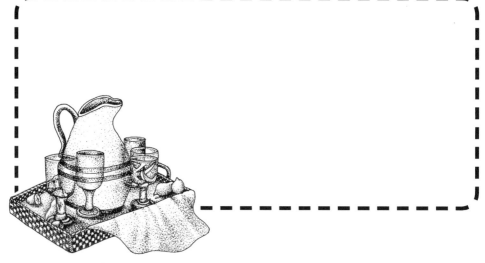

Date-Pineapple Bran Muffins
Instructions for baking:
1 egg, slightly beaten
$1/4$ cup vegetable oil
$1/3$ cup milk
1 (8 ounce) can crushed pineapple with juice

1. Preheat oven to 400°.
2. Empty contents of jar into large bowl and stir to mix.
3. In separate bowl, combine egg, vegetable oil, milk and pineapple with juice and blend well.
4. Add liquid mixture to dry mixture and set aside for 5 minutes to soften bran.
5. Continue stirring just until mixture blends.
6. Spoon batter into 12 prepared muffin cups.
7. Bake for 20 minutes or until tester comes out clean.

www.cookbookresources.com

Date-Pineapple Bran Muffins
Instructions for baking:
1 egg, slightly beaten
$1/4$ cup vegetable oil
$1/3$ cup milk
1 (8 ounce) can crushed pineapple with juice

1. Preheat oven to 400°.
2. Empty contents of jar into large bowl and stir to mix.
3. In separate bowl, combine egg, vegetable oil, milk and pineapple with juice and blend well.
4. Add liquid mixture to dry mixture and set aside for 5 minutes to soften bran.
5. Continue stirring just until mixture blends.
6. Spoon batter into 12 prepared muffin cups.
7. Bake for 20 minutes or until tester comes out clean.

www.cookbookresources.com

Date-Pineapple Bran Muffins
Instructions for baking:
1 egg, slightly beaten
$1/4$ cup vegetable oil
$1/3$ cup milk
1 (8 ounce) can crushed pineapple with juice

1. Preheat oven to 400°.
2. Empty contents of jar into large bowl and stir to mix.
3. In separate bowl, combine egg, vegetable oil, milk and pineapple with juice and blend well.
4. Add liquid mixture to dry mixture and set aside for 5 minutes to soften bran.
5. Continue stirring just until mixture blends.
6. Spoon batter into 12 prepared muffin cups.
7. Bake for 20 minutes or until tester comes out clean.

www.cookbookresources.com

Light and Fluffy Cinnamon Muffins

Light and Fluffy Cinnamon Muffins

Ingredients for Jar:
3 cups flour
1 tablespoon baking powder
1 teaspoon salt
1 cup sugar
1 teaspoon cinnamon

Instructions for Jar:
1. Combine flour with baking powder and salt.

2. Spoon into bottom of 1-quart jar.

3. In separate bowl, combine sugar and cinnamon and mix
   thoroughly.

4. Spoon cinnamon mixture over flour mixture.

5. Place lid on jar, close and attach baking instructions.

♥ Decorate your jar using the suggestions found
   on pages 4 and 5.

Light and Fluffy Cinnamon Muffins

Instructions for baking:

⅔ cup butter, melted
2 eggs, slightly beaten
1 cup milk

1. Preheat oven to 350°.

2. Spoon contents of jar into large bowl and stir to mix.

3. In separate bowl, whisk melted butter, eggs and milk and blend well.

4. Add liquid mixture to dry mixture and stir just until moist.

5. Spoon batter into 12 prepared muffin cups.

6. Bake for 20 to 25 minutes or until tester comes out clean.

Note: This recipe makes 24 muffins. If you want to make 12 muffins now and 12 later, cut the ingredients in half.

"The human race has one really effective weapon, and that is laughter."
~Mark Twain

Light and Fluffy Cinnamon Muffins

Instructions for baking:
²/₃ cup butter, melted
2 eggs, slightly beaten
1 cup milk

1. Preheat oven to 350°.
2. Spoon contents of jar into large bowl and stir to mix.
3. In separate bowl, whisk melted butter, eggs and milk and blend well.
4. Add liquid mixture to dry mixture and stir just until moist.
5. Spoon batter into 12 prepared muffin cups.
6. Bake for 20 to 25 minutes or until tester comes out clean.

Note: This recipe makes 24 muffins. If you want to make 12 muffins now and 12 later, cut the ingredients in half.

www.cookbookresources.com

- -

Light and Fluffy Cinnamon Muffins

Instructions for baking:
²/₃ cup butter, melted
2 eggs, slightly beaten
1 cup milk

1. Preheat oven to 350°.
2. Spoon contents of jar into large bowl and stir to mix.
3. In separate bowl, whisk melted butter, eggs and milk and blend well.
4. Add liquid mixture to dry mixture and stir just until moist.
5. Spoon batter into 12 prepared muffin cups.
6. Bake for 20 to 25 minutes or until tester comes out clean.

Note: This recipe makes 24 muffins. If you want to make 12 muffins now and 12 later, cut the ingredients in half.

www.cookbookresources.com

- -

Light and Fluffy Cinnamon Muffins

Instructions for baking:
²/₃ cup butter, melted
2 eggs, slightly beaten
1 cup milk

1. Preheat oven to 350°.
2. Spoon contents of jar into large bowl and stir to mix.
3. In separate bowl, whisk melted butter, eggs and milk and blend well.
4. Add liquid mixture to dry mixture and stir just until moist.
5. Spoon batter into 12 prepared muffin cups.
6. Bake for 20 to 25 minutes or until tester comes out clean.

Note: This recipe makes 24 muffins. If you want to make 12 muffins now and 12 later, cut the ingredients in half.

www.cookbookresources.com

Light and Fluffy Cinnamon Muffins
Instructions for baking:
$^2/_3$ cup butter, melted
2 eggs, slightly beaten
1 cup milk

1. Preheat oven to 350°.
2. Spoon contents of jar into large bowl and stir to mix.
3. In separate bowl, whisk melted butter, eggs and milk and blend well.
4. Add liquid mixture to dry mixture and stir just until moist.
5. Spoon batter into 12 prepared muffin cups.
6. Bake for 20 to 25 minutes or until tester comes out clean.

Note: This recipe makes 24 muffins. If you want to make 12 muffins now and 12 later, cut the ingredients in half.

Light and Fluffy Cinnamon Muffins
Instructions for baking:
$^2/_3$ cup butter, melted
2 eggs, slightly beaten
1 cup milk

1. Preheat oven to 350°.
2. Spoon contents of jar into large bowl and stir to mix.
3. In separate bowl, whisk melted butter, eggs and milk and blend well.
4. Add liquid mixture to dry mixture and stir just until moist.
5. Spoon batter into 12 prepared muffin cups.
6. Bake for 20 to 25 minutes or until tester comes out clean.

Note: This recipe makes 24 muffins. If you want to make 12 muffins now and 12 later, cut the ingredients in half.

www.cookbookresources.com

Light and Fluffy Cinnamon Muffins
Instructions for baking:
$^2/_3$ cup butter, melted
2 eggs, slightly beaten
1 cup milk

1. Preheat oven to 350°.
2. Spoon contents of jar into large bowl and stir to mix.
3. In separate bowl, whisk melted butter, eggs and milk and blend well.
4. Add liquid mixture to dry mixture and stir just until moist.
5. Spoon batter into 12 prepared muffin cups.
6. Bake for 20 to 25 minutes or until tester comes out clean.

Note: This recipe makes 24 muffins. If you want to make 12 muffins now and 12 later, cut the ingredients in half.

www.cookbookresources.com

Spicy Bran Muffins

Spicy Bran Muffins

Ingredients for Jar:

2 cups bran cereal
$1^1/_4$ cups flour
2 teaspoons baking powder
1 teaspoon baking soda
$1/_2$ teaspoon salt
$1/_2$ cup packed brown sugar
$1/_4$ cup sugar
$1^1/_2$ teaspoons cinnamon

Instructions for Jar:

1. Spoon bran cereal into bottom of 1-quart jar.

2. Combine flour with baking powder, baking soda and salt. Spoon over bran cereal.

3. Layer brown sugar evenly over flour mixture.

4. Combine sugar with cinnamon and mix thoroughly. Spoon over brown sugar.

5. Place lid on jar, close and attach baking directions.

♥ Decorate your jar using the suggestions found on pages 4 and 5.

Spicy Bran Muffins

Instructions for baking:

1¹/₄ cups milk
¹/₃ cup vegetable oil
2 eggs, slightly beaten

1. Preheat oven to 375°.

2. Empty contents of jar into large bowl and stir to mix.

3. In separate bowl, whisk milk, vegetable oil and eggs and blend well.

4. Add liquid mixture to dry mixture and stir to blend well. Set aside for 5 minutes to soften bran.

5. Spoon batter into 12 prepared muffin cups.

6. Bake for 15 to 20 minutes or until tester comes out clean.

"Not everything that can be counted counts and not everything that counts can be counted."
~Albert Einstein

Spicy Bran Muffins
Instructions for baking:
1¹/₄ cups milk
¹/₃ cup vegetable oil
2 eggs, slightly beaten

1. Preheat oven to 375°.
2. Empty contents of jar into large bowl and stir to mix.
3. In separate bowl, whisk milk, vegetable oil and eggs and blend well.
4. Add liquid mixture to dry mixture and stir to blend well. Set aside for 5 minutes to soften bran.
5. Spoon batter into 12 prepared muffin cups.
6. Bake for 15 to 20 minutes or until tester comes out clean.

www.cookbookresources.com

Spicy Bran Muffins
Instructions for baking:
1¹/₄ cups milk
¹/₃ cup vegetable oil
2 eggs, slightly beaten

1. Preheat oven to 375°.
2. Empty contents of jar into large bowl and stir to mix.
3. In separate bowl, whisk milk, vegetable oil and eggs and blend well.
4. Add liquid mixture to dry mixture and stir to blend well. Set aside for 5 minutes to soften bran.
5. Spoon batter into 12 prepared muffin cups.
6. Bake for 15 to 20 minutes or until tester comes out clean.

www.cookbookresources.com

Spicy Bran Muffins
Instructions for baking:
1¹/₄ cups milk
¹/₃ cup vegetable oil
2 eggs, slightly beaten

1. Preheat oven to 375°.
2. Empty contents of jar into large bowl and stir to mix.
3. In separate bowl, whisk milk, vegetable oil and eggs and blend well.
4. Add liquid mixture to dry mixture and stir to blend well. Set aside for 5 minutes to soften bran.
5. Spoon batter into 12 prepared muffin cups.
6. Bake for 15 to 20 minutes or until tester comes out clean.

Spicy Bran Muffins
Instructions for baking:
1¹/₄ cups milk
¹/₃ cup vegetable oil
2 eggs, slightly beaten

1. Preheat oven to 375°.
2. Empty contents of jar into large bowl and stir to mix.
3. In separate bowl, whisk milk, vegetable oil and eggs and blend well.
4. Add liquid mixture to dry mixture and stir to blend well. Set aside for 5 minutes to soften bran.
5. Spoon batter into 12 prepared muffin cups.
6. Bake for 15 to 20 minutes or until tester comes out clean.

www.cookbookresources.com

Spicy Bran Muffins
Instructions for baking:
1¹/₄ cups milk
¹/₃ cup vegetable oil
2 eggs, slightly beaten

1. Preheat oven to 375°.
2. Empty contents of jar into large bowl and stir to mix.
3. In separate bowl, whisk milk, vegetable oil and eggs and blend well.
4. Add liquid mixture to dry mixture and stir to blend well. Set aside for 5 minutes to soften bran.
5. Spoon batter into 12 prepared muffin cups.
6. Bake for 15 to 20 minutes or until tester comes out clean.

www.cookbookresources.com

Spicy Bran Muffins
Instructions for baking:
1¹/₄ cups milk
¹/₃ cup vegetable oil
2 eggs, slightly beaten

1. Preheat oven to 375°.
2. Empty contents of jar into large bowl and stir to mix.
3. In separate bowl, whisk milk, vegetable oil and eggs and blend well.
4. Add liquid mixture to dry mixture and stir to blend well. Set aside for 5 minutes to soften bran.
5. Spoon batter into 12 prepared muffin cups.
6. Bake for 15 to 20 minutes or until tester comes out clean.

Pecan-Butterscotch Muffins

Pecan-Butterscotch Muffins

Ingredients for Jar:

2 cups quick cooking oats
3/4 cup packed brown sugar
1 cup flour
1 1/2 teaspoons baking powder
1/2 teaspoon salt
1/2 teaspoon baking soda
1/2 cup butterscotch chips

Instructions for Jar:

1. Spoon oats into bottom of 1-quart jar.

2. Layer brown sugar evenly over oats.

3. Combine flour with baking powder, salt and baking soda. Spoon over brown sugar.

4. Spoon butterscotch chips over flour mixture.

5. Place lid on jar, close and attach baking instructions.

♥ Decorate your jar using the suggestions found on pages 4 and 5.

Pecan-Butterscotch Muffins

Instructions for baking:

1 ¹/₃ cups buttermilk
¹/₂ cup (1 stick) butter, melted
2 eggs, slightly beaten

1. Preheat oven to 400°.

2. Empty contents of jar into large bowl and stir to mix.

3. In separate bowl, whisk buttermilk, melted butter and eggs.

4. Add liquid mixture to dry mixture and stir just until moist.

5. Spoon batter into 12 prepared muffin cups.

6. Bake for 15 to 20 minutes or until tester comes out clean.

Tip: To make buttermilk, mix 1 cup milk with 1 tablespoon lemon juice
   or vinegar and set aside for about 10 minutes.

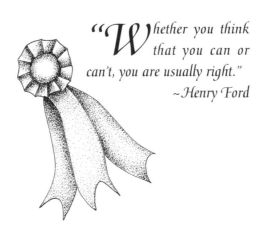

*"Whether you think
that you can or
can't, you are usually right."
~Henry Ford*

Pecan-Butterscotch Muffins
Instructions for baking:
1 ¹/₃ cups buttermilk
¹/₂ cup (1 stick) butter, melted
2 eggs, slightly beaten

1. Preheat oven to 400°.
2. Empty contents of jar into large bowl and stir to mix.
3. In separate bowl, whisk buttermilk, melted butter and eggs.
4. Add liquid mixture to dry mixture and stir just until moist.
5. Spoon batter into 12 prepared muffin cups.
6. Bake for 15 to 20 minutes or until tester comes out clean.
Tip: To make buttermilk, mix 1 cup milk with 1 tablespoon lemon juice or vinegar and set aside
     for about 10 minutes.

www.cookbookresources.com

Pecan-Butterscotch Muffins
Instructions for baking:
1 ¹/₃ cups buttermilk
¹/₂ cup (1 stick) butter, melted
2 eggs, slightly beaten

1. Preheat oven to 400°.
2. Empty contents of jar into large bowl and stir to mix.
3. In separate bowl, whisk buttermilk, melted butter and eggs.
4. Add liquid mixture to dry mixture and stir just until moist.
5. Spoon batter into 12 prepared muffin cups.
6. Bake for 15 to 20 minutes or until tester comes out clean.
Tip: To make buttermilk, mix 1 cup milk with 1 tablespoon lemon juice or vinegar and set aside
     for about 10 minutes.

www.cookbookresources.com

Pecan-Butterscotch Muffins
Instructions for baking:
1 ¹/₃ cups buttermilk
¹/₂ cup (1 stick) butter, melted
2 eggs, slightly beaten

1. Preheat oven to 400°.
2. Empty contents of jar into large bowl and stir to mix.
3. In separate bowl, whisk buttermilk, melted butter and eggs.
4. Add liquid mixture to dry mixture and stir just until moist.
5. Spoon batter into 12 prepared muffin cups.
6. Bake for 15 to 20 minutes or until tester comes out clean.
Tip: To make buttermilk, mix 1 cup milk with 1 tablespoon lemon juice or vinegar and set aside
     for about 10 minutes.

www.cookbookresources.com

Pecan-Butterscotch Muffins
Instructions for baking:
1 $1/3$ cups buttermilk
$1/2$ cup (1 stick) butter, melted
2 eggs, slightly beaten

1. Preheat oven to 400°.
2. Empty contents of jar into large bowl and stir to mix.
3. In separate bowl, whisk buttermilk, melted butter and eggs.
4. Add liquid mixture to dry mixture and stir just until moist.
5. Spoon batter into 12 prepared muffin cups.
6. Bake for 15 to 20 minutes or until tester comes out clean.

Tip: To make buttermilk, mix 1 cup milk with 1 tablespoon lemon juice or vinegar and set aside for about 10 minutes.

www.cookbookresources.com

- -

Pecan-Butterscotch Muffins
Instructions for baking:
1 $1/3$ cups buttermilk
$1/2$ cup (1 stick) butter, melted
2 eggs, slightly beaten

1. Preheat oven to 400°.
2. Empty contents of jar into large bowl and stir to mix.
3. In separate bowl, whisk buttermilk, melted butter and eggs.
4. Add liquid mixture to dry mixture and stir just until moist.
5. Spoon batter into 12 prepared muffin cups.
6. Bake for 15 to 20 minutes or until tester comes out clean.

Tip: To make buttermilk, mix 1 cup milk with 1 tablespoon lemon juice or vinegar and set aside for about 10 minutes.

www.cookbookresources.com

- -

Pecan-Butterscotch Muffins
Instructions for baking:
1 $1/3$ cups buttermilk
$1/2$ cup (1 stick) butter, melted
2 eggs, slightly beaten

1. Preheat oven to 400°.
2. Empty contents of jar into large bowl and stir to mix.
3. In separate bowl, whisk buttermilk, melted butter and eggs.
4. Add liquid mixture to dry mixture and stir just until moist.
5. Spoon batter into 12 prepared muffin cups.
6. Bake for 15 to 20 minutes or until tester comes out clean.

Tip: To make buttermilk, mix 1 cup milk with 1 tablespoon lemon juice or vinegar and set aside for about 10 minutes.

www.cookbookresources.com

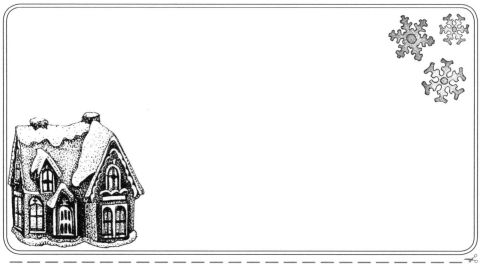

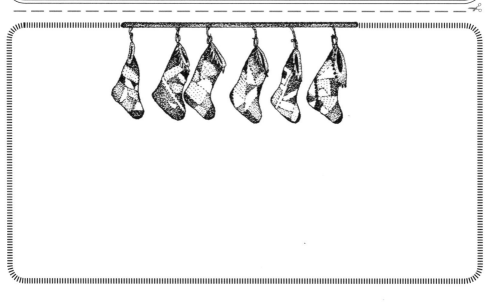

Lemon Poppy Seed Muffins

Lemon Poppy Seed Muffins

Ingredients for Jar:
1 ⅓ cups sugar
2 ⅔ cups flour
2 teaspoons baking powder
1 teaspoon baking soda
4 tablespoons poppy seeds
4 tablespoons dried lemon rind
1 teaspoon salt

Instructions for Jar:

1. Put sugar in bottom of 1-quart jar.

2. Combine flour with baking powder, baking soda, poppy seeds, lemon rind and salt.

3. Spoon flour mixture over sugar.

4. Put lid on jar, close and attach baking instructions.

♥ Decorate your jar using the suggestions found on pages 4 and 5.

Lemon Poppy Seed Muffins

Instructions for baking:

4 eggs, slightly beaten
1 cup (2 sticks) butter, melted
1 cup buttermilk
2 teaspoons vanilla

1. Preheat oven to 350°.

2. Empty contents of jar into large bowl and stir to mix.

3. In separate bowl, whisk eggs, melted butter, buttermilk and vanilla and blend well.

4. Add liquid mixture into dry mixture and stir lightly just until moist.

5. Spoon batter into 12 prepared muffin cups.

6. Bake for 20 to 25 minutes or until tester comes out clean.

Note: This recipe makes 24 muffins. If you want to make 12 muffins now and 12 later, cut the ingredients in half.

"I have not failed. I've just found 100,000 ways that won't work."
~Thomas Alva Edison

Lemon Poppy Seed Muffins
Instructions for baking:
4 eggs, slightly beaten
1 cup (2 sticks) butter, melted
1 cup buttermilk
2 teaspoons vanilla

1. Preheat oven to 350°.
2. Empty contents of jar into large bowl and stir to mix.
3. In separate bowl, whisk eggs, melted butter, buttermilk and vanilla and blend well.
4. Add liquid mixture into dry mixture and stir lightly just until moist.
5. Spoon batter into 12 prepared muffin cups.
6. Bake for 20 to 25 minutes or until tester comes out clean.

Lemon Poppy Seed Muffins
Instructions for baking:
4 eggs, slightly beaten
1 cup (2 sticks) butter, melted
1 cup buttermilk
2 teaspoons vanilla

1. Preheat oven to 350°.
2. Empty contents of jar into large bowl and stir to mix.
3. In separate bowl, whisk eggs, melted butter, buttermilk and vanilla and blend well.
4. Add liquid mixture into dry mixture and stir lightly just until moist.
5. Spoon batter into 12 prepared muffin cups.
6. Bake for 20 to 25 minutes or until tester comes out clean.

Lemon Poppy Seed Muffins
Instructions for baking:
4 eggs, slightly beaten
1 cup (2 sticks) butter, melted
1 cup buttermilk
2 teaspoons vanilla

1. Preheat oven to 350°.
2. Empty contents of jar into large bowl and stir to mix.
3. In separate bowl, whisk eggs, melted butter, buttermilk and vanilla and blend well.
4. Add liquid mixture into dry mixture and stir lightly just until moist.
5. Spoon batter into 12 prepared muffin cups.
6. Bake for 20 to 25 minutes or until tester comes out clean.

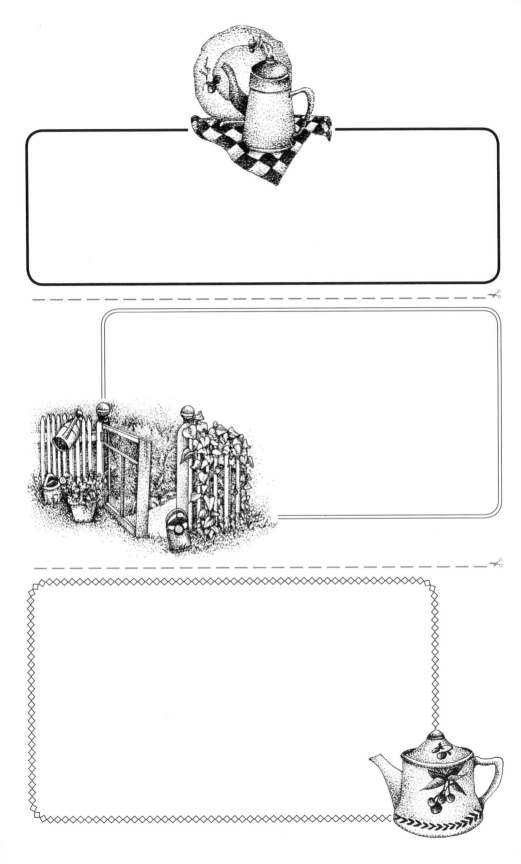

Lemon Poppy Seed Muffins
Instructions for baking:
4 eggs, slightly beaten
1 cup (2 sticks) butter, melted
1 cup buttermilk
2 teaspoons vanilla

1. Preheat oven to 350°.
2. Empty contents of jar into large bowl and stir to mix.
3. In separate bowl, whisk eggs, melted butter, buttermilk and vanilla and blend well.
4. Add liquid mixture into dry mixture and stir lightly just until moist.
5. Spoon batter into 12 prepared muffin cups.
6. Bake for 20 to 25 minutes or until tester comes out clean.

www.cookbookresources.com

Lemon Poppy Seed Muffins
Instructions for baking:
4 eggs, slightly beaten
1 cup (2 sticks) butter, melted
1 cup buttermilk
2 teaspoons vanilla

1. Preheat oven to 350°.
2. Empty contents of jar into large bowl and stir to mix.
3. In separate bowl, whisk eggs, melted butter, buttermilk and vanilla and blend well.
4. Add liquid mixture into dry mixture and stir lightly just until moist.
5. Spoon batter into 12 prepared muffin cups.
6. Bake for 20 to 25 minutes or until tester comes out clean.

www.cookbookresources.com

Lemon Poppy Seed Muffins
Instructions for baking:
4 eggs, slightly beaten
1 cup (2 sticks) butter, melted
1 cup buttermilk
2 teaspoons vanilla

1. Preheat oven to 350°.
2. Empty contents of jar into large bowl and stir to mix.
3. In separate bowl, whisk eggs, melted butter, buttermilk and vanilla and blend well.
4. Add liquid mixture into dry mixture and stir lightly just until moist.
5. Spoon batter into 12 prepared muffin cups.
6. Bake for 20 to 25 minutes or until tester comes out clean.

www.cookbookresources.com

Healthy Wheat-Germ Muffins

Healthy Wheat-Germ Muffins

Ingredients for Jar:
1 cup wheat germ
$1^1/_2$ cups flour
2 teaspoons baking powder
1 teaspoon salt
$^1/_4$ cup sugar
$^1/_2$ cup chopped nuts
1 cup sweetened, shredded coconut

Instructions for Jar:

1. Place wheat germ in bottom of 1-quart jar.

2. Combine flour with baking powder and salt. Spoon evenly over wheat germ.

3. Spoon sugar over flour.

4. Layer nuts and coconut over sugar and press down gently to fit.

5. Place lid on jar, close and attach baking instructions.

Healthy Wheat-Germ Muffins

Instructions for baking:

1 egg, slightly beaten
$^3/_4$ cup milk
$^1/_4$ cup ($^1/_2$ stick) butter, melted
$^1/_4$ cup molasses

1. Preheat oven to 400°.

2. Empty contents of jar into large bowl and stir to mix.

3. In separate bowl, whisk egg, milk, melted butter and molasses.

4. Add liquid mixture to dry mixture and stir just until moist.

5. Spoon batter into 12 prepared muffin cups.

6. Bake for 20 minutes or until brown on top.

"There are only two ways to live your life. One is as though nothing is a miracle. The other is as though everything is a miracle."

~Albert Einstein

Healthy Wheat-Germ Muffins
Instructions for baking:
1 egg, slightly beaten
$^3/_4$ cup milk
$^1/_4$ cup ($^1/_2$ stick) butter, melted
$^1/_4$ cup molasses

1. Preheat oven to 400°.
2. Empty contents of jar into large bowl and stir to mix.
3. In separate bowl, whisk egg, milk, melted butter and molasses.
4. Add liquid mixture to dry mixture and stir just until moist.
5. Spoon batter into 12 prepared muffin cups.
6. Bake for 20 minutes or until brown on top.

www.cookbookresources.com

Healthy Wheat-Germ Muffins
Instructions for baking:
1 egg, slightly beaten
$^3/_4$ cup milk
$^1/_4$ cup ($^1/_2$ stick) butter, melted
$^1/_4$ cup molasses

1. Preheat oven to 400°.
2. Empty contents of jar into large bowl and stir to mix.
3. In separate bowl, whisk egg, milk, melted butter and molasses.
4. Add liquid mixture to dry mixture and stir just until moist.
5. Spoon batter into 12 prepared muffin cups.
6. Bake for 20 minutes or until brown on top.

www.cookbookresources.com

Healthy Wheat-Germ Muffins
Instructions for baking:
1 egg, slightly beaten
$^3/_4$ cup milk
$^1/_4$ cup ($^1/_2$ stick) butter, melted
$^1/_4$ cup molasses

1. Preheat oven to 400°.
2. Empty contents of jar into large bowl and stir to mix.
3. In separate bowl, whisk egg, milk, melted butter and molasses.
4. Add liquid mixture to dry mixture and stir just until moist.
5. Spoon batter into 12 prepared muffin cups.
6. Bake for 20 minutes or until brown on top.

www.cookbookresources.com

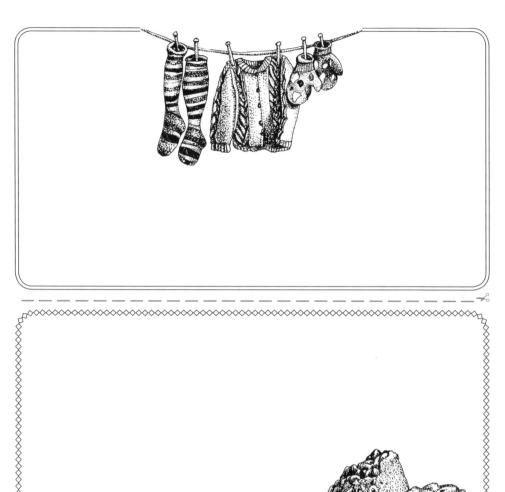

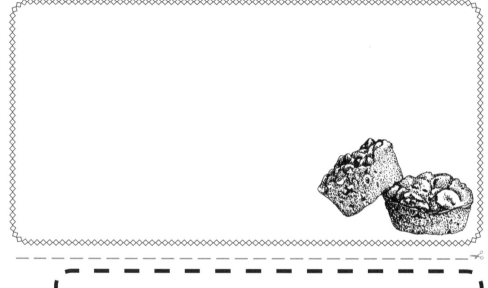

Healthy Wheat-Germ Muffins
Instructions for baking:
1 egg, slightly beaten
$^3/_4$ cup milk
$^1/_4$ cup ($^1/_2$ stick) butter, melted
$^1/_4$ cup molasses

1. Preheat oven to 400°.
2. Empty contents of jar into large bowl and stir to mix.
3. In separate bowl, whisk egg, milk, melted butter and molasses.
4. Add liquid mixture to dry mixture and stir just until moist.
5. Spoon batter into 12 prepared muffin cups.
6. Bake for 20 minutes or until brown on top.

www.cookbookresources.com

Healthy Wheat-Germ Muffins
Instructions for baking:
1 egg, slightly beaten
$^3/_4$ cup milk
$^1/_4$ cup ($^1/_2$ stick) butter, melted
$^1/_4$ cup molasses

1. Preheat oven to 400°.
2. Empty contents of jar into large bowl and stir to mix.
3. In separate bowl, whisk egg, milk, melted butter and molasses.
4. Add liquid mixture to dry mixture and stir just until moist.
5. Spoon batter into 12 prepared muffin cups.
6. Bake for 20 minutes or until brown on top.

www.cookbookresources.com

Healthy Wheat-Germ Muffins
Instructions for baking:
1 egg, slightly beaten
$^3/_4$ cup milk
$^1/_4$ cup ($^1/_2$ stick) butter, melted
$^1/_4$ cup molasses

1. Preheat oven to 400°.
2. Empty contents of jar into large bowl and stir to mix.
3. In separate bowl, whisk egg, milk, melted butter and molasses.
4. Add liquid mixture to dry mixture and stir just until moist.
5. Spoon batter into 12 prepared muffin cups.
6. Bake for 20 minutes or until brown on top.

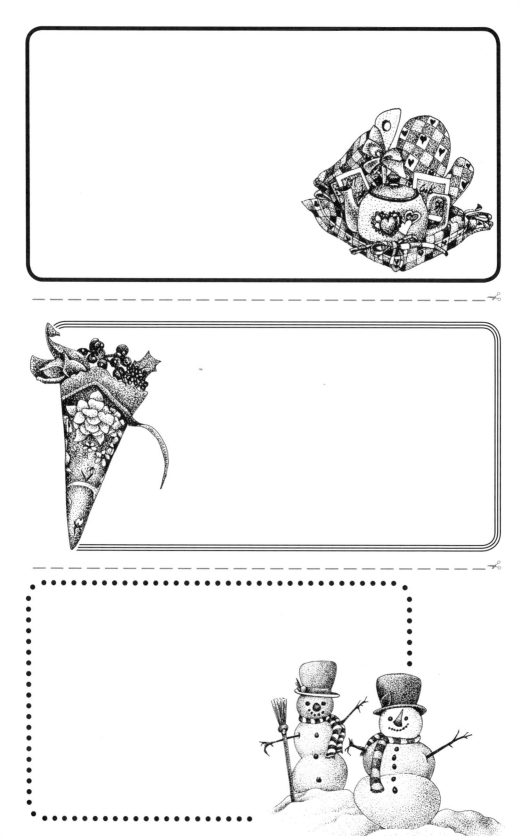

Spicy Applesauce-Nut Muffins

Spicy Applesauce-Nut Muffins

Ingredients for Jar:
2 cups dry biscuit and baking mix
$^1/_2$ cup sugar
$1^1/_2$ teaspoons cinnamon
1 cup coarsely chopped walnuts
$^1/_2$ cup raisins

Instructions for Jar:
1. Pour biscuit mix in bottom of 1-quart jar.

2. In separate bowl, combine sugar with cinnamon and mix thoroughly.

3. Spoon sugar mixture evenly over biscuit mix.

4. Place walnuts over sugar mixture and top with raisins.

5. Place lid on jar, close and attach baking instructions.

♥ Decorate your jar using the suggestions found on pages 4 and 5.

Spicy Applesauce-Nut Muffins

Instructions for baking:

$^1/_2$ cup applesauce
$^1/_4$ cup milk
1 egg, slightly beaten
$^1/_4$ cup (4 tablespoons) butter, melted

1. Preheat oven to 400°.

2. Empty contents of jar into large bowl and stir to mix.

3. In separate bowl, whisk applesauce, milk, egg and melted butter and blend well.

4. Add liquid mixture to dry mixture and stir just until mixture is moist.

5. Spoon batter into 12 prepared muffin cups.

6. Bake for 12 to 15 minutes or until golden brown.

"Refrain from asking what is going to happen tomorrow and everyday that fortune grants you, count as gain."

~Horace

Spicy Applesauce-Nut Muffins

Instructions for baking:

$^1/_2$ cup applesauce
$^1/_4$ cup milk
1 egg, slightly beaten
$^1/_4$ cup (4 tablespoons) butter, melted

1. Preheat oven to 400°.
2. Empty contents of jar into large bowl and stir to mix.
3. In separate bowl, whisk applesauce, milk, egg and melted butter and blend well.
4. Add liquid mixture to dry mixture and stir just until mixture is moist.
5. Spoon batter into 12 prepared muffin cups.
6. Bake for 12 to 15 minutes or until golden brown.

www.cookbookresources.com

Spicy Applesauce-Nut Muffins

Instructions for baking:

$^1/_2$ cup applesauce
$^1/_4$ cup milk
1 egg, slightly beaten
$^1/_4$ cup (4 tablespoons) butter, melted

1. Preheat oven to 400°.
2. Empty contents of jar into large bowl and stir to mix.
3. In separate bowl, whisk applesauce, milk, egg and melted butter and blend well.
4. Add liquid mixture to dry mixture and stir just until mixture is moist.
5. Spoon batter into 12 prepared muffin cups.
6. Bake for 12 to 15 minutes or until golden brown.

www.cookbookresources.com

Spicy Applesauce-Nut Muffins

Instructions for baking:

$^1/_2$ cup applesauce
$^1/_4$ oup milk
1 egg, slightly beaten
$^1/_4$ cup (4 tablespoons) butter, melted

1. Preheat oven to 400°.
2. Empty contents of jar into large bowl and stir to mix.
3. In separate bowl, whisk applesauce, milk, egg and melted butter and blend well.
4. Add liquid mixture to dry mixture and stir just until mixture is moist.
5. Spoon batter into 12 prepared muffin cups.
6. Bake for 12 to 15 minutes or until golden brown.

www.cookbookresources.com

Spicy Applesauce-Nut Muffins
Instructions for baking:
$^1/_2$ cup applesauce
$^1/_4$ cup milk
1 egg, slightly beaten
$^1/_4$ cup (4 tablespoons) butter, melted

1. Preheat oven to 400°.
2. Empty contents of jar into large bowl and stir to mix.
3. In separate bowl, whisk applesauce, milk, egg and melted butter and blend well.
4. Add liquid mixture to dry mixture and stir just until mixture is moist.
5. Spoon batter into 12 prepared muffin cups.
6. Bake for 12 to 15 minutes or until golden brown.

www.cookbookresources.com

Spicy Applesauce-Nut Muffins
Instructions for baking:
$^1/_2$ cup applesauce
$^1/_4$ cup milk
1 egg, slightly beaten
$^1/_4$ cup (4 tablespoons) butter, melted

1. Preheat oven to 400°.
2. Empty contents of jar into large bowl and stir to mix.
3. In separate bowl, whisk applesauce, milk, egg and melted butter and blend well.
4. Add liquid mixture to dry mixture and stir just until mixture is moist.
5. Spoon batter into 12 prepared muffin cups.
6. Bake for 12 to 15 minutes or until golden brown.

www.cookbookresources.com

Spicy Applesauce-Nut Muffins
Instructions for baking:
$^1/_2$ cup applesauce
$^1/_4$ cup milk
1 egg, slightly beaten
$^1/_4$ cup (4 tablespoons) butter, melted

1. Preheat oven to 400°.
2. Empty contents of jar into large bowl and stir to mix.
3. In separate bowl, whisk applesauce, milk, egg and melted butter and blend well.
4. Add liquid mixture to dry mixture and stir just until mixture is moist.
5. Spoon batter into 12 prepared muffin cups.
6. Bake for 12 to 15 minutes or until golden brown.

www.cookbookresources.com

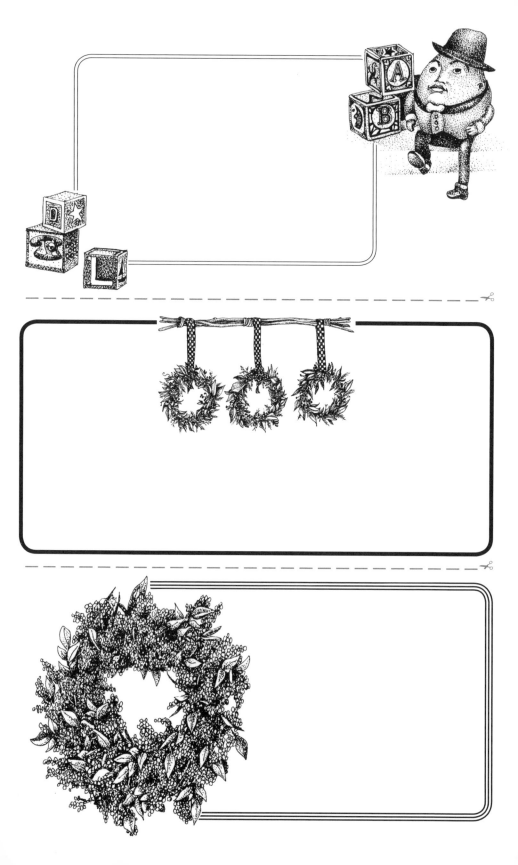

Nutty Apricot Muffins

Nutty Apricot Muffins

Ingredients for Jar:
2 cups flour
2 teaspoons baking powder
$1/2$ teaspoon salt
1 cup finely chopped, dried apricots
$3/4$ cup sugar
$1/2$ cup chopped pecans or almonds

Instructions for Jar:
1. Combine flour with baking powder and salt. Spoon into bottom of 1-quart jar.

2. Layer apricots over flour mixture.

3. Layer sugar over apricots, then top with pecans.

4. Place lid on jar, close and attach baking instructions.

♥ Decorate your jar using the suggestions found on pages 4 and 5.

Nutty Apricot Muffins

Instructions for baking:

1/2 cup (1 stick) butter, melted
1 egg, slightly beaten
1 cup buttermilk

1. Preheat oven to 400°.

2. Empty contents of jar into large bowl and stir to mix.

3. In separate bowl, whisk melted butter, egg and buttermilk.

4. Add liquid mixture to dry mixture and stir until just moist.

5. Spoon batter into 12 prepared muffin cups.

6. Bake for 15 to 18 minutes or until tester comes out clean.

Tip: To make buttermilk, mix 1 cup milk and 1 tablespoon lemon juice or
vinegar and set aside for about 10 minutes.

" Always laugh when you can.
It is cheap medicine."
~Lord Byron

Nutty Apricot Muffins

Instructions for baking:
¹/₂ cup (1 stick) butter, melted
1 egg, slightly beaten
1 cup buttermilk

1. Preheat oven to 400°.
2. Empty contents of jar into large bowl and stir to mix.
3. In separate bowl, whisk melted butter, egg and buttermilk.
4. Add liquid mixture to dry mixture and stir until just moist.
5. Spoon batter into 12 prepared muffin cups.
6. Bake for 15 to 18 minutes or until tester comes out clean.

Tip: To make buttermilk, mix 1 cup milk and 1 tablespoon lemon juice or vinegar and set aside
    for about 10 minutes.

www.cookbookresources.com

- ✂

Nutty Apricot Muffins

Instructions for baking:
¹/₂ cup (1 stick) butter, melted
1 egg, slightly beaten
1 cup buttermilk

1. Preheat oven to 400°.
2. Empty contents of jar into large bowl and stir to mix.
3. In separate bowl, whisk melted butter, egg and buttermilk.
4. Add liquid mixture to dry mixture and stir until just moist.
5. Spoon batter into 12 prepared muffin cups.
6. Bake for 15 to 18 minutes or until tester comes out clean.

Tip: To make buttermilk, mix 1 cup milk and 1 tablespoon lemon juice or vinegar and set aside
    for about 10 minutes.

www.cookbookresources.com

- ✂

Nutty Apricot Muffins

Instructions for baking:
¹/₂ cup (1 stick) butter, melted
1 egg, slightly beaten
1 cup buttermilk

1. Preheat oven to 400°.
2. Empty contents of jar into large bowl and stir to mix.
3. In separate bowl, whisk melted butter, egg and buttermilk.
4. Add liquid mixture to dry mixture and stir until just moist.
5. Spoon batter into 12 prepared muffin cups.
6. Bake for 15 to 18 minutes or until tester comes out clean.

Tip: To make buttermilk, mix 1 cup milk and 1 tablespoon lemon juice or vinegar and set aside
    for about 10 minutes.

www.cookbookresources.com

Nutty Apricot Muffins
Instructions for baking:
$^1/_2$ cup (1 stick) butter, melted
1 egg, slightly beaten
1 cup buttermilk

1. Preheat oven to 400°.
2. Empty contents of jar into large bowl and stir to mix.
3. In separate bowl, whisk melted butter, egg and buttermilk.
4. Add liquid mixture to dry mixture and stir until just moist.
5. Spoon batter into 12 prepared muffin cups.
6. Bake for 15 to 18 minutes or until tester comes out clean.

Tip: To make buttermilk, mix 1 cup milk and 1 tablespoon lemon juice or vinegar and set aside
    for about 10 minutes.

- ✂

Nutty Apricot Muffins
Instructions for baking:
$^1/_2$ cup (1 stick) butter, melted
1 egg, slightly beaten
1 cup buttermilk

1. Preheat oven to 400°.
2. Empty contents of jar into large bowl and stir to mix.
3. In separate bowl, whisk melted butter, egg and buttermilk.
4. Add liquid mixture to dry mixture and stir until just moist.
5. Spoon batter into 12 prepared muffin cups.
6. Bake for 15 to 18 minutes or until tester comes out clean.

Tip: To make buttermilk, mix 1 cup milk and 1 tablespoon lemon juice or vinegar and set aside
    for about 10 minutes.

www.cookbookresources.com

- ✂

Nutty Apricot Muffins
Instructions for baking:
$^1/_2$ cup (1 stick) butter, melted
1 egg, slightly beaten
1 cup buttermilk

1. Preheat oven to 400°.
2. Empty contents of jar into large bowl and stir to mix.
3. In separate bowl, whisk melted butter, egg and buttermilk.
4. Add liquid mixture to dry mixture and stir until just moist.
5. Spoon batter into 12 prepared muffin cups.
6. Bake for 15 to 18 minutes or until tester comes out clean.

Tip: To make buttermilk, mix 1 cup milk and 1 tablespoon lemon juice or vinegar and set aside
    for about 10 minutes.

www.cookbookresources.com

Graham Cracker Muffins

Graham Cracker Muffins

Ingredients for Jar:
$^1/_2$ cup packed brown sugar
1 cup graham cracker crumbs
1 cup flour
1 teaspoon baking powder
$^1/_2$ teaspoon salt
1 cup sweetened, shredded coconut
$^3/_4$ cup chocolate chips

Instructions for Jar:
1. Place brown sugar in bottom of 1-quart jar.

2. Spoon graham cracker crumbs over brown sugar.

3. Combine flour with baking powder and salt. Spoon evenly over graham cracker crumbs.

4. Layer coconut over graham cracker crumbs and top with chocolate chips.

5. Place lid on jar, close and attach baking instructions.

♥ Decorate your jar using the suggestions found on pages 4 and 5.

Graham Cracker Muffins

Instructions for baking:

2 eggs, slightly beaten
1 cup milk
$^{1}/_{4}$ cup ($^{1}/_{2}$ stick) butter, melted
$^{1}/_{4}$ cup applesauce

1. Preheat oven to 400°.

2. Empty contents of jar into large bowl and stir to mix.

3. In separate bowl, whisk eggs, milk, melted butter and applesauce.

4. Add liquid mixture to dry mixture and stir just until they blend.

5. Spoon batter into 12 prepared muffin cups.

6. Bake for 20 to 25 minutes or until tester comes out clean.

" Cherish all your happy moments: they make a fine cushion for old age."
~ Christopher Morley

Graham Cracker Muffins
Instructions for baking:
2 eggs, slightly beaten
1 cup milk
$^1/_4$ cup ($^1/_2$ stick) butter, melted
$^1/_4$ cup applesauce

1. Preheat oven to 400°.
2. Empty contents of jar into large bowl and stir to mix.
3. In separate bowl, whisk eggs, milk, melted butter and applesauce.
4. Add liquid mixture to dry mixture and stir just until they blend.
5. Spoon batter into 12 prepared muffin cups.
6. Bake for 20 to 25 minutes or until tester comes out clean.

www.cookbookresources.com

Graham Cracker Muffins
Instructions for baking:
2 eggs, slightly beaten
1 cup milk
$^1/_4$ cup ($^1/_2$ stick) butter, melted
$^1/_4$ cup applesauce

1. Preheat oven to 400°.
2. Empty contents of jar into large bowl and stir to mix.
3. In separate bowl, whisk eggs, milk, melted butter and applesauce.
4. Add liquid mixture to dry mixture and stir just until they blend.
5. Spoon batter into 12 prepared muffin cups.
6. Bake for 20 to 25 minutes or until tester comes out clean.

www.cookbookresources.com

Graham Cracker Muffins
Instructions for baking:
2 eggs, slightly beaten
1 cup milk
$^1/_4$ cup ($^1/_2$ stick) butter, melted
$^1/_4$ cup applesauce

1. Preheat oven to 400°.
2. Empty contents of jar into large bowl and stir to mix.
3. In separate bowl, whisk eggs, milk, melted butter and applesauce.
4. Add liquid mixture to dry mixture and stir just until they blend.
5. Spoon batter into 12 prepared muffin cups.
6. Bake for 20 to 25 minutes or until tester comes out clean.

www.cookbookresources.com

Graham Cracker Muffins

Instructions for baking:
2 eggs, slightly beaten
1 cup milk
$1/4$ cup ($1/2$ stick) butter, melted
$1/4$ cup applesauce

1. Preheat oven to 400°.
2. Empty contents of jar into large bowl and stir to mix.
3. In separate bowl, whisk eggs, milk, melted butter and applesauce.
4. Add liquid mixture to dry mixture and stir just until they blend.
5. Spoon batter into 12 prepared muffin cups.
6. Bake for 20 to 25 minutes or until tester comes out clean.

Graham Cracker Muffins

Instructions for baking:
2 eggs, slightly beaten
1 cup milk
$1/4$ cup ($1/2$ stick) butter, melted
$1/4$ cup applesauce

1. Preheat oven to 400°.
2. Empty contents of jar into large bowl and stir to mix.
3. In separate bowl, whisk eggs, milk, melted butter and applesauce.
4. Add liquid mixture to dry mixture and stir just until they blend.
5. Spoon batter into 12 prepared muffin cups.
6. Bake for 20 to 25 minutes or until tester comes out clean.

Graham Cracker Muffins

Instructions for baking:
2 eggs, slightly beaten
1 cup milk
$1/4$ cup ($1/2$ stick) butter, melted
$1/4$ cup applesauce

1. Preheat oven to 400°.
2. Empty contents of jar into large bowl and stir to mix.
3. In separate bowl, whisk eggs, milk, melted butter and applesauce.
4. Add liquid mixture to dry mixture and stir just until they blend.
5. Spoon batter into 12 prepared muffin cups.
6. Bake for 20 to 25 minutes or until tester comes out clean.

Muffins In A Jar Gift Reference

Date	Name of Recipient	Name of Muffin Given

COOKBOOKS PUBLISHED BY COOKBOOK RESOURCES, LLC

The Ultimate Cooking With 4 Ingredients
Easy Cooking With 5 Ingredients
The Best of Cooking With 3 Ingredients
Easy Gourmet-Style Cooking With 5 Ingredients
Gourmet Cooking With 5 Ingredients
Healthy Cooking With 4 Ingredients
Diabetic Cooking With 4 Ingredients
Easy Dessert Cooking With 5 Ingredients
4-Ingredient Recipes And 30-Minute Meals
Easy Slow-Cooker Cooking
Quick Fixes With Cake Mixes
Casseroles To The Rescue
Holiday Recipes
Kitchen Keepsakes/More Kitchen Keepsakes
Mother's Recipes
Recipe Keepsakes
Cookie Dough Secrets
Gifts For The Cookie Jar
Brownies In A Jar
Muffins In A Jar
101 Best Brownies
Cookie Jar Magic
Quilters' Cooking Companion
Classic Southern Cooking
Classic Tex-Mex and Texas Cooking
Classic Southwest Cooking
Classic Pennsylvania-Dutch Cooking
Classic New England Cooking
The Great Canadian Cookbook
The Best of Lone Star Legacy Cookbook
Lone Star Legacy
Lone Star Legacy II
Cookbook 25 Years
Pass The Plate
Authorized Texas Ranger Cookbook
Texas Longhorn Cookbook
Trophy Hunters' Guide To Cooking
Mealtimes and Memories
Homecoming
Little Taste of Texas
Little Taste of Texas II
Texas Peppers
Southwest Sizzler
Southwest Ole
Class Treats
Leaving Home

cookbook
resources LLC

To Order Muffins In A Jar:

Please send_____copies @ $9.95 (U.S.) each $_____

Plus postage/handling @ $6.00 for first book $_____

and $1.00 for each additional book $_____

Texas residents add sales tax @ $ .80 each $_____

Check or Credit Card (Canada-credit card only)   TOTAL $_____

Charge to my   ❏ Master Card   or   ❏ Visa Card

Account #_____

Expiration Date_____

Signature_____

Name_____

Address_____

City_____State_____Zip_____

Phone (day)_____ (night)_____

Mail or Call:
Cookbook Resources
541 Doubletree Dr.
Highland Village, Texas 75077
Toll Free (866) 229-2665
(972) 317-6404 Fax
www.cookbookresources.com

- -

To Order Muffins In A Jar:

Please send_____copies @ $9.95 (U.S.) each $_____

Plus postage/handling @ $6.00 for first book $_____

and $1.00 for each additional book $_____

Texas residents add sales tax @ $ .80 each $_____

Check or Credit Card (Canada-credit card only)   TOTAL $_____

Charge to my   ❏ Master Card   or   ❏ Visa Card

Account #_____

Expiration Date_____

Signature_____

Name_____

Address_____

City_____State_____Zip_____

Phone (day)_____ (night)_____

Mail or Call:
Cookbook Resources
541 Doubletree Dr.
Highland Village, Texas 75077
Toll Free (866) 229-2665
(972) 317-6404 Fax
www.cookbookresources.com